Good Water

Good Water

KEVIN HOLDSWORTH

UNIVERSITY PRESS OF COLORADO
Boulder

© 2016 by Kevin J. Holdsworth

Published by University Press of Colorado
5589 Arapahoe Avenue, Suite 206C
Boulder, Colorado 80303

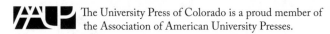 The University Press of Colorado is a proud member of
the Association of American University Presses.

The University Press of Colorado is a cooperative publishing enterprise supported, in part, by Adams State University, Colorado State University, Fort Lewis College, Metropolitan State University of Denver, Regis University, University of Colorado, University of Northern Colorado, Utah State University, and Western State Colorado University.

∞ This paper meets the requirements of the ANSI/NISO Z39.48-1992 (Permanence of Paper).

ISBN: 978-1-60732-454-6 (pbk)
ISBN: 978-1-60732-455-3 (ebook)
DOI: 10.5876/9781607324553

Library of Congress Cataloging-in-Publication Data

Holdsworth, Kevin.
  Good Water / Kevin Holdsworth.
    pages cm
  ISBN 978-1-60732-454-6 (paperback : alkaline paper) — ISBN 978-1-60732-455-3 (ebook)
  1. Torrey (Utah)—History. 2. Torrey (Utah)—Social life and customs. 3. Torrey (Utah)—Biography. 4. Holdsworth, Kevin—Homes and haunts—Utah—Torrey. 5. Land use—Utah—Torrey. 6. Water-supply—Utah—Torrey. 7. Torrey (Utah)—Environmental conditions. I. Title.
  F834.T67H65 2016
  979.2'54—dc23

                    2015013782

25 24 23 22 21 20 19 18 17 16   10 9 8 7 6 5 4 3 2 1

Cover photograph © Guy Tal

For Jennifer

Contents

CONTENTS

CEDAR AND STONE

To grow among stone? Nobody's goal.
But if the wind or water leaves you there
or the road traveled stops, you grow.

—KEN BREWER, *SMALL SCENES*

Prelude

WINTER LIGHT

They can look two hundred miles, clear into Colorado; and looking down over the cliffs and canyons of the San Rafael Swell and the Robber's Roost they can also look as deeply into themselves as anywhere I know.
　　—Wallace Stegner, "Wilderness Letter," 1964

Don Juan, my amigo of long standing, and I are sitting at 10,000 feet on black boulders poking up through cast-iron snow on a minor ridge on the southeast corner of Boulder Mountain, Utah. We had hoped to come up here to ski, to yo-yo a few runs above Spruce Spring, but the snow is hard as a sidewalk, with a little death crust blown in, so to get down we will do something like skiing: survival skiing, a slapstick, risky business. Still, we'll trade bad skiing for a grand view anytime.

We are dressed in full winter regalia. It's the last day of 2007. The air temperature stands at a bracing 6°. A brass-brassiere breeze out of the southwest at three to seven knots ensures that we will not be able to look into ourselves for too long. This is a manly afternoon out. We left our loved ones down in the valley: his Christy, my Jennifer and Christopher.

As flat-topped mountains go, Boulder is among the biggest in North America. It has many slopes, sides, and ends, and each has its particular character. This southeast end was only lightly glaciated and expresses itself in open rolling meadows, vast stands of aspen, and thick-growing groves of spruce and fir. Marked for our time by catastrophic fires a century ago, the patterns of meadow and forest resemble an overo pony.

Boulder is handsome in itself, but what extends below sets it apart: the entire western edge of the Colorado Plateau, an enormous expanse of wasteland country, laid out this afternoon in polychromatic clarity.

The last few days of high wind have scoured the power plant pollution from the air. No forest fires are burning. This view extends farthest in winter. Wallace Stegner may have exaggerated in the epigraph above, but you can certainly see 150 miles today, clear to Colorado and beyond.

The warm color of the escarpments and mesas below contrast nicely with the snowy slopes of Boulder and the niveous cones of the Henry Mountains. Each rock formation has a name and a lengthy history. We recite stratigraphy: Moenkopi, Chinle, Wingate, Kayenta, Navajo, Entrada, Morrison, Mancos Shale. We bother to name the closer landforms—there's San Rafael, Caineville Mesa, Factory Butte, Tarantula Mesa, Bloody Hands Gap, Circle Cliffs—and point out the farther ones as well: Book Cliffs, Roan Cliffs, La Sal Mountains, Uncompahgre, Abajo, Bears Ears. Names control the chaos, turn it down a little. There isn't a town of any size out there. Nor bodies of water, either, wider than the bottom of a canyon.

If I take off my glasses, the escarpments de-focus into stripes of color, big gaudy bell-bottomed '70s-style stripes, and what a variegation: buff whites, creamy whites, bleached-bone whites, and grays topped with ochers, and golds mixed with blues, and browns and duns and cinnabars and cinnamons, siennas and umbers, vermilions and raw earths, and two dozen reds: brick red, sunburn red, rose madder red, commie-star red, pinkish red, salsa red, ruby red, blowsy red, stop-sign red.

Today's special is the Boulder Combo Plate: warm-hued earth, dark mountain trees, pearly snow slopes, *azul* sky—a home planet pattern to remember.

As we admire this exceptional American view, as grand as the National Mall in April, New York Harbor on the Fourth of July, or the Golden Gate in October, Don Juan says, "You are weak and conceited, Kevin."

I am. Don Juan is in much better physical condition. He trains daily, obsessively: hiking, running, riding his bicycle up hills. And as for conceit, mine is richly colored.

"Yes, and that makes me worried about the way down, Don Juan. There's much tensegrity in the snowpack. Tensegrity, dude . . . Death must be our advisor, death or at least serious injury."

He nods. He grimaces. He looks away. Danger.

Don Juan works in Capitol Reef National Park and lives in the employee housing known as the Fish Bowl. Living there, he gets to know everyone's business, and everyone his. Don Juan works as the cultural resources manager. He manages to protect the Fremont Culture ruins and artifacts by not telling the public where they are and shines more light on the Mormon homesteader relic orchards. Some days he manages to walk around armed with a clipboard. Because he's a good hand, fit, steady, and trained, he participates in park rescues: plucking stuck, scared pilgrims from ledges and cliffs. He also spends quite a bit of time online looking for his next federal employment opportunity.

Don Juan looks remarkably like Clint Eastwood in his *Pale Rider* or *Josey Wales* periods, although a few pounds lighter and generally without the menacing stare and bad personal habits. I've known him for twenty-five years, and I'll admit that for a portion of that time I've wanted to kill him. Particularly on countless backcountry trips when I've been exasperated by his practice of "not doing," especially with group work or equipment or thinking about the needs of others. He has had a karmic imbalance.

"You, too, are weak and conceited, Don Juan. Weak. Conceited."

"I guess I am. But I've been working on it." He flips a ski pole. "Say, there *is* tensegrity in the snowpack."

And yet, for all the conflicted times, we have shared many great days of idyllic rambling and rapt contemplation: overlooking the Hudson River from Riverside Park, walking beside sixty-three perfect lakes in the Wind Rivers in September, and wilding with the spirits at the Great Overhang on Velvet Ridge. For much of this time, Don Juan has been a searcher, a rolling stone.

"The purpose of existence for all sentient beings is to enhance awareness," he says.

"You know it is. Also good to enhance awareness is skiing in season."

It's easier to roll when single. Roots can be hard to sink in Wayne County. The land is harsh and the people can be hostile. There's little for diversion. Living in a place like the Fish Bowl can make a person long to get away.

Not wanting to host or fund a party, Don Juan and Christy recently slunk over to Colorado to get married on the sly at Powderhorn near Grand Junction. They needed no preacher. It's a bit odd, sure, but to be a good friend, I toast the unexpected nuptials, as well as his new bride, with minis of Jack and Jim.

"Here's to you, Don Juan, and it's about time you made that warrior-princess an honest woman."

He looks thoughtful. "Power comes only after we accept our fate," he swigs. "Acceptance is the beginning of wisdom." He swigs again and winces. "The beginning of wisdom."

We remember to toast Bill Clinton, whose masterstroke had nothing to do with destroying the deficit or the Dayton Accords. It lies below us: the Grand Staircase-Escalante National Monument, declared in 1996, a pandering to the bicoastal elites that protected the southern reaches of this big, big view from a host of bad uses, a blessed kind of accident that changed everything in this part of the world. Here's to you, Bill!

Our lingering has left us cold. Now we must go down to the valley below.

"Practice not falling," Don Juan reminds as we fasten skis for the scary descent.

Really bad skiing is perhaps better than no skiing, but today's conditions take really bad skiing to the next level. There's the Boulder Mountain Pavement: rock-hard, icy, hollow-sounding snow. Mixed in is some good old-fashioned Death Crust: firmish layers of crust over deep pockets of sugary, weak snow. When Death Crust gives way, and it does, the skis plunge, the skier lunges, and the skier enjoys a snow snack. This unexpected forward motion is hard on joints, ligaments, spinal alignment, and pride.

Perhaps with downhill gear these conditions would not be as dire, but we have donned our old-school leather boots, svelte skis, and no-heeled bindings for today's exploration by fair means.

"Always remember this is the place where you will die," Don Juan shouts as he pushes off.

"Tensegrity, bro!. Death be your advisor!"

We ski down defensively: poles up and facing out in anticipation of a booby trap. We traverse gingerly and make kick turns.

Don Juan and I are baby boomers; tailenders, true, but boomers to be sure. All the leaves are brown. Out on the open slopes my feet wiggle like Mama Cass in her white go-go boots trying to find purchase on the hellish snow. I pretend to pray.

He ends up far ahead of me. No surprise. To walk or ski with Don Juan is to walk or ski alone. When I finally reach the road, though, I'm filled with the intense warrior pleasure of survival: no lacy tracks or pleasurable yo-yo, just being alive.

The ruddy wasteland below glows. It does and does not beckon.

Some people come here to hide, just as they did in the outlaw days. Some are attracted to the freedom the edge provides. Some disappear, following the routes of the Old People. Some go down into the ledges and never return. There's something out there that pulls you away and into the chaos of the canyons. Something out there makes leaving it all behind easy enough to do.

Good Water

Introduction

HANTAVIRUS

I ROUGH-FRAMED THIS SHED WITHOUT USING power tools over one snowy and two clearer but windy days in March 1988. I was twenty-seven and really had no idea what I was doing. The reason I chose to put up a shed was monetary, or rather the lack of monetary. The shed was to become a summertime honeymoon shack. My fiancée, Dora, and I were going to start work on a cabin following our June wedding and needed a place to live. A tent wasn't going to provide enough comfort. I checked into used travel trailers, but after living in one for eight weeks, we'd be stuck with a used travel trailer and no way to pull it away. No, I figured that with about $300 worth of lumber, some tools borrowed from my father, and a little time and trouble, I could construct something that would at least keep the rain out. Another plus was that it reminded me of a Talking Heads song. I wanted to find myself living in a shotgun shack.

It wasn't exactly roughing it. The shed stood on an acre and a half within the limits of Good Water, Utah, population 126. Electricity was provided by a construction post that featured two outstanding twenty-amp circuits. A frost-free hookup to the municipal water system furnished all the spring water a person could drink, and with a hose and a utility sink baling-wired to an old pole fence, we could wash clothes, dishes, and hands. A wooden table, a canvas tarp for a sun shade, a propane camp stove, lawn chairs, loud music as needed, a cooler, a short walk to the Arm and Leg General Store—all these conveniences made it almost civilized for modern-day homesteaders.

Good Water is located on a broad, lightly sloping expanse called Poverty Flat on the map. The town's first name was Poverty Bench. This moniker was subsequently changed to Bonita, which was an attempt to put a smiley face on the poverty. Later it gained the appellation Torrey, either from John C. Fremont's botanist or one of Teddy Roosevelt's Rough Riders, one Colonel Torrey, depending on whom you believe. Later still, the several-named town became Good Water for transparent reasons.

I dug a hole for an outdoor commode and used cast-off squirrely new boards and several bad old planks to enclose it. Open to the south, it offered an estimable view. There were no neighbors in that direction. I filled a Kmart kiddie pool with water each morning, covered it with clear polyethylene during the day, and by evening the water was warm enough for a dip. I took my bath, naked in the field. Dora showered at the Arm and Leg Kampground.

The shed, eight feet by twelve, was not much smaller than Thoreau's digs at Walden Pond. The bed was a platform four feet off the floor. The shed was never meant to be more than temporary lodging while we built a proper domicile. Since we only had eight free weeks to dig a foundation, build floor and walls, put the roof on, install windows and doors, and get the cabin closed in, we were under a great deal of pressure to get things done.

This was called a working vacation. This should have been called a bad idea. Pressure led to physical exhaustion, tension, and trouble. But hey, you're only young once, although you may be foolish many times.

Dora and I built half a house together but our marriage eventually fell apart.

—

The first Good Waterite I met was a woman in her eighties named Jet Smith. She lived on the property just north of our homestead. I was digging the outhouse hole, down deep in my work, aiming for China, when I heard a shrill voice, looked up, and saw an elderly woman leaning on the sheep fence, wielding a cane. She resembled an owl.

"What you doin'?" She said it in a curious, nonthreatening way. She poked at the grass with her cane. She introduced herself, Dorthy Jenette Hickman Smith, "but you can call me Jet."

I told her I was just digging a hole.

"Well, you'll need plenty of those."

We got to talking. Jet had grown up in nearby Grover but had moved to Good Water around 1920 with her husband Walt. They lived twelve years in a 20 x 24 building that they built themselves, a garage really, and raised their two sons, Dow and Wayne. I had bought our lot from Wayne.

She told me that they raised livestock. At first they had sheep, then later cattle—fewer but worth more. They had grazing allotments on the east end of Boulder Mountain for the summer and out on Beas Lewis Flat in the winter. They owned the whole parcel from where we stood to the Fremont River, which they used for pasturing and hay. Eventually they were able to build the larger house that Jet still occupied, a winsome ranch-roofed structure surrounded by tall spruce, with a porch that opened onto the Good Water Canal. The house was sided in red and green to match the landscape.

Walt had worked for years to install the municipal water system and served several terms as mayor. The current mayor, Jay Chestnut, was "a no-good pup" who had always taken credit for Walt's work. Walt had passed away just a few months previously. I told her I was sorry. She said, "He was getting kind of old at the end." He had died at ninety-six.

Jet looked around. Her bottle-bottom glasses magnified her gray eyes. "You know, Good Water's the prettiest town in the *whole* country. There's a red cliff up there on *my* mountain, and when it rains it looks like it's covered with diamonds." She made an ample gesture and then continued, "Walt and I traveled around quite a bit after we retired. I say *we* because Walt wasn't a bad man—he just worked me nearly to death. Work, work, work. If you've got the livestock, why, then, you've sure got the work.

"We seen Washington, D.C., New York City, other places. Went to the Chicago World's Fair. Those places are fine, but Good Water's the prettiest. But the people," she said, looking down at her cane, "whew!"

She told me I could stop by anytime and left me to my work.

—

Sometimes I hate this shed and want to tear it down, reuse what I can, and start again. Recycle it. It's not that I regret having a shed. Everyone needs one for storing junk and tools, but the design bothers me because it's too simple, too primitive, too back then, and the way I built it leaves room for improvement and space for mice.

Deer mice and field mice have called the honeymoon shack home. Mice are carriers of hantavirus, an affliction that begins with flulike symptoms and can lead, if untreated, quite quickly to the cemetery. Hantavirus has been found throughout this part of Utah as well as the entire Southwest. People are infected by hantavirus by inhaling spores from mouse turds and dried urine. One of the easiest ways to inhale deadly spores is by cleaning out sheds and other unventilated, seldom-used buildings. The precautions are widely known and easy to follow: spray the offending areas with a mixture of bleach and water, wear an OSHA-approved mask, and don disposable gloves. Putting out mice or rat poison, too, is a good preventative measure.

Mice wiggle their way into the shed, set up shop, and leave toxic party favors that resemble caraway seeds. Some of them die from the poison, and I discover their dried remains behind things, smelling them first. In this way, as in many others, the shed has always been a place to locate things I might not want to find.

The worst part is that it's nobody's fault but my own. The design, I mean. The way I threw up the shed and cobbled it together. Construction is bad that way: you build your mistakes right in and have to look at them always. If I knew then what I know now . . .

Still, to tear down a perfectly useful shed seems a bit extreme, and building a dreamland shed would take time and money I don't have.

Because this shed houses certain regrets of personal history, it's a regrettable shed of regrets. It sheds and keeps the rain off my regrets, keeps them dry, if mousy. Many of us have both a regrettable shed and a shed of regrets. Even when we move away we leave these sheds behind.

A mask, gloves, and Clorox work on mice waste, but will they work on memories?

—

What is trash and what is junk? What do you save and what do you throw away?

In the early days you took your household trash to the city dump yourself. There was no weekly visit from the county's waste transport truck. The Good Water dump, located on a little knoll south of town, was notable for several reasons. The site offered a bracing view: right down the gullet of the Fremont Gorge, to the bulge of Miner's Mountain, over the tops of the Waterpocket Fold, and to the Henry Mountains beyond.

Visiting was always an adventure. With half a century of refuse there, it was nearly always possible to find something of interest at the dump, particularly the farther east you roamed. The dump had its own wildlife, primarily ravens, *Corvus corax*, as well as a few feral cats. The ravens could be seen flying over Poverty Flat in the late afternoons and early mornings. Ravens are social birds and enjoyed their communal visiting no less than their rotten vegetables. The birds scavenged widely but must have known where they could find reliable and safe sustenance.

The nocturnal dump bonfires, lit in flagrant violation of several ordinances, provided special effects, particularly when someone had brought in an old corral, fence, or shed and it was possible to see the twenty-foot-high flames from town. The illegal burning of garbage and whatnot obviated the need for more landfill space.

Human scavenging was winked at, even smiled upon in those days, back when Poverty Flat was still poor. Sure, it might be embarrassing to be seen loading up some old posts for firewood or discarded sheep fence or whatever, but almost everyone did it. I got most of the material for the roof for another outbuilding by scooping up and hauling back cast-off wafer board pieces from the construction of a local motel, the Egyptian.

Decentralized recycling was in full swing at the old dump. There was a special section where you could leave useful items for others: old furniture and primitive computers, outgrown bicycles, boxes of books or clothes, no-longer-needed shelving, and so on.

As for carbon-based things that were not directly recyclable, the flesh pit provided a place for those: cows, horses, sheep, dogs, cats, llamas, and goats in various states of decomposition. A parade of horrors.

Finally, there were a great many free and pretty rocks at the dump, rocks that could be used to build an unmortared rock wall or decorate a garden. Jet Smith used to watch me bring back loads of rocks and remark, "Lard, we spent years haulin' them rocks out of that pasture. And now you're haulin' 'em back!"

Recycling.

—

Five generations of my family have lived in Utah along the Wasatch Front, from Cache Valley on the north to Utah Valley on the south. My great-great-grandparents, all of them, crossed the plains in the 1850s and 1860s as part of the Mormon migration from the dispossessed classes of Europe, mainly English but also Danish and German. Although not among the first wave to settle Salt Lake City, and therefore not among the Mormon royalty, nevertheless they founded or settled some towns, most notably Logan, Smithfield, and Richmond, and their roots were sunk in the agrarian towns that grew at the foot of mountains where there was plentiful water and deep soil.

None of them had any inclination to settle sunburned southern Utah. Few others did.

Whether Good Water is located in Utah or in its own special vortex is the subject of some debate. Torrey's Knoll is widely known as the Cosmic Navel of the Universe. It even shows up on GPS as such.

I remember when Leon Chappell referred to visiting Provo as "Driving up into Utah." As far as that goes, Wayne County has always been a bit off the beaten. To drop into the county there is the choice of three mountain passes over 8,300 feet or the snake-twist route through the Waterpocket Fold.

This country was settled lightly and late. Good Water was first inhabited in 1888, exactly 100 years before I built the shed and cabin. Far-flung County.

Good Water has always been marked by its outlaw past. The homesteader who first claimed this side of town was Robert Lee, son of John D. Lee of Mountain Meadows Massacre fame. John D. Lee was the "fall guy" for this atrocity, in which, by ruse and trickery, over 120 men, women, and children—members of a California-bound emigrant train—were murdered by Mormon settlers at Mountain Meadows in Iron County. (Another interesting connection: John D. Lee had also served a mission and converted the "notorious" Wild Bill Hickman, one of Brigham Young's hit men and Jet Smith's great-grandfather.) Robert Lee (the Lee clan came from Kentucky) had two brothers who found small-time trouble with the law, Charlie and Rains Lee, though Charlie Lee, known as Char Lee, later went straight and even appears in Wallace Stegner's *Mormon Country.*

The openness to diversity extends to this day: no one faith has a majority in Good Water. The buildings of three different denominations stand in town: Latter-Day Saint, Southern Baptist, and Catholic, a rarity in tiny-town south-central Utah.

Coming at the very tail end of the hippie reinhabitation, I immediately sensed that this place was well beyond the gray blandishments of the Zion Curtain. Mayor Jay Chestnut explained, "There's a lot of us around here can't seem to make it to Sunday school, son."

Things have changed. I remember the early days when the cemetery was not surrounded by two motels, two convenience stores, an RV park, a go-cart track, and a B and B; before the art galleries and gift shops; back when the fly fishing boutique was actually a gas station; when the town dump was not prime real estate; when the Clean and Quiet Motel still sported a large windmill out front from its salad days as the Little Holland; and before the annual Red Rock Women's Music Festival, now a major stop on the alternative Euterpean circuit. No, I arrived before this Old West turned new and there still existed some remnants of the frontier culture.

—

Twenty years have passed since I built the shed. This is the right time for some dedicated purging. I'll be able to fill the property-of-Wayne-County-do-not-remove-under-penalty-of-law black poly dumpster on wheels with some of the stuff, but it's clear that one or two loads of bulkier junk will have to be hauled to the new county landfill, located in a sagey, windswept hollow uphill from Loa, twenty miles away, no scavenging allowed. I'll pile the stuff in a small utility trailer hitched to the back of the big beautiful Dodge. I'll try not to look back to see what might be left scattered on the road.

Years of living here off and on can amount to quite a collection of personal detritus: various and sundry guano that has accumulated on the platform that once served as a bed.

I need storage space for my splendid selection of American-made power tools. I've been working on the cabin again and need a dry, secure place to store the tools until I can tackle the next project, a little hut for my son, Christopher.

—

The key to purging, as with so many monotonous and essentially physical tasks, is momentum—rhythm and mojo. It's the same way you climb up the sandstone around here. You get on a roll and go with the mo. You best not stop. *I hope that flake don't break.* Here, too, it's easier to be hard-hearted and less sentimental when you're tuned up and rocking. Don't think, just toss.

My paternal grandfather, William Jonas Holdsworth, used to save nails. He worked as a mail carrier—after many lean years—and also worked a few acres of poor land, but he was frugal, not to say stingy, as anyone from his generation, Jet Smith's generation, learned to be. I recall times when he would accompany us to my father's cattle ranch in Indianola, Utah. My grandmother Isabel would pack a lunch bucket that featured Depression sandwiches: thin-sliced Spam with mayonnaise on homemade cracked-wheat bread and Cragmont sodas bought by the dozen from Safeway. After lunch, Grandpa Bill would use the bucket to collect bent and cast-off nails and junk. He puttered on various small construction projects, especially in a large building we called simply the Big Barn. Invariably he would bring home a pail of nails. No old board was safe from him. We'd hear the squeak of the crowbar or thud of a hammer and the tinkle of another treasure in the bucket. The nails Grandpa Bill brought home would be transferred to other buckets of nails in his dusty barn, and the junk would be stored for some unknown future use.

My father, Jay, was also a secret storer of nails, though I know he tried to keep the hoarding from my mother, for whom everything about the cattle ranch was disgusting, unkempt, and dirty. I know he saved them, though. I remember two buckets filled with rusty bent nails that he kept in his own shed beside the carport. Jay had seen his father spend an hour at a time—no more, and only on a rainy day, since there were always things that needed doing—straightening those nails against the future. How could the future be rosy when the past had included the crash of '29, Hitler, and that darned socialist FDR? As I say, my father stored buckets of old nails, but I'm not sure that he straightened them.

It is for this reason, among others, that I have a hard time throwing things away. For one thing, it's twenty tedious miles to Loa and the hardware store when you need a special flange, mounting escutcheon, maniform coupler, or flux capacitor, and when you don't have one, or can't figure out a way to make do with what you have, nothing interferes with the mojo more than the drive to Loa. Loa, just say no-a.

Busy and impatient, my father never seemed to have enough time to do all the jobs he made for himself, but he persisted with a kind of sweaty-browed perversity just to show whatever he was battling who was boss. If I didn't inherit his practicality or his devotion to work, I follow his lead in this way: despite long bouts of indolence, when the mania kicks in, it's difficult for me to let go of it. So kindly get out of the way and don't ask any questions.

So it is with junk. Sawn-through extension cords, cracked irrigation boots, first-wedding photographs, outdated correspondence, broken ski goggles, a fan encrusted with mouse turds, dish-drying racks, gummed-up paintbrushes, bent nails, stripped bolts, cans of old paint, dead mice, papers from school, papers from work, papers papers papers—all of it gets tossed in the utility trailer.

Some decisions are simple. Others are tough. Old Red doesn't pass the test. A mountain bike from the Ordovician Period, Old Red was in sad shape when I got him secondhand, with slightly bent front forks and not the best of brakes. Still, there are as many memories as pieces of duct tape on the trusty red steed: the time I carried Old Red for hours—yes, hours—hopelessly lost in the thick aspen above Chris Lake; the time friends Bob, Joanne, and I rode, pushed (and also simply steered while walking behind and trying to hold on) down the steep and rocky "trail" off the south slope of Thousand Lake Mountain, a day that led to Joanne's voluntary early retirement from high-adventure mountain bike "riding" and should have led to mine.

I will lash Old Red on top of my dump-bound pile, where it will be an anchor for the rest. At the dump I'll toss Old Red in with the furniture and tree branches and old carpet, and I will not look back. Seeing the sorrow in my eyes, my lovely wife, Jennifer, promises to buy me a new bicycle, a so-called comfort bicycle. A two-wheeled way to form a bridge between long-lost youth and the golden years. Golden years? Don't let me hear you say life's taking you nowhere, Angel. The only good place for "middle age" is in the dump, too. Well . . .

Part One

Moving Water

NEIGHBORS SHOULDN'T BE TOO GOOD. How are you going to recompense all those home-cooked meals, plates of cookies, valuable stories, every favor large or small? You can't. I'm not saying neighbors should be bad, either—it's just easier to deal with people in between. Plus, things change. People move or pass away. Too-good neighbors leave too-large gaps, as my first Good Water neighbors did. Both Jet Smith and Doug Wells were relicts, fossils from an earlier time, and both made a natural span between the ways things are and how they used to be.

Doug Wells grew up in Hanksville. His nephew, LaVar Wells, still digs wells for a living out of that sandblasted town where the Fremont River meets Muddy Creek and becomes the Dirty Devil. Doug himself dug wells, drove trucks, gathered firewood, punched cattle, and did a dozen other jobs in his time. Mainly what he wanted to do in his late fifties, when I knew him, was to raise a few cattle. Not because it made any economic sense. It didn't. But because that's what he knew, what he wanted to know. He shuttled his critters between Good Water and his home at the mouth of Weber Canyon, near Ogden. He also had a winter grazing allotment east of Hite, in the Cheesebox-White Canyon country, but the road was damned rough down there, the feed scarce most years, the water pockets just dried up, and the predators plumb brazen.

Doug and I had an unspoken competition to see who could get up the earliest and work the hardest. Dawn would find him out in the pasture moving water, irrigating. Mornings he'd repair some equipment or run errands. Afternoons he spent making furniture or working on his cabin. Evenings he'd find something to do, under floodlights if he had to. He beat me hands down, even with a three-decade head start.

Work is both righteous and inevitable. There's something about this land that makes you overdo it, a toehold mentality. You gaze around yourself and see nothing but wilderness: wide-stretching mountains, sun-baked canyons and mesas, moony badlands, and you'd like to do your part to domesticate your little quarter. Also there is the problem of the weather, particularly the wind: five thousand feet of vertical relief makes for some full-on shaking and rattling. Faced with a raging world out of control, you want to batten down what you can after a three-day blow.

Doug Wells was more than just a manic rancher. It doesn't take any élan to work hard. He was also an artist cowboy. He wrote good cowboy poetry. At the end of the day, when the work was done, he liked nothing better than to set on his back porch, abuse a guitar, and sing to his cattle when no one was looking, listening. Sometimes the critters were gentled by his song. Other times they milled restlessly and probably begrudged his high-pitched coyote wail. When he warbled "Red River Valley," let me tell you, he meant it.

I've never seen anyone irrigate with such determination. Water is blood to a desert cowboy. When the ditch water was flowing onto his land, he wouldn't let it pool up, coagulate too long. Nothing much to it, he'd say: put on your boots, get down into your work, and keep it moving. Six days on the ditch, six days off—just enough to transfuse fifty acres of pasture. He irrigated during snowstorms and during the rain. I believe he went out there late at night, checking head gates, fixing dams.

You know how sometimes people resemble their dogs or vice versa? With Doug it was horses. He owned one very stuck-up open mare that wouldn't even give you the time of day when her owner was around. But one time, when he was away, I went over to give Miss Hoity-Toity an apple. It was spooky: she had the same wrinkles over the eyes, the same bulldog neck, the same perpetual sunburn, the same sly grin, even the same laconic manner as Doug.

It is in the cowboy manner to understate, the it's-just-a-flesh-wound, git-back-on-the-horse-that-bucked-ya-off, tough-guy mentality. True, there are times when cowboys tend to overstate, but usually Doug's lingo tended toward the minimal and dry. After I built a seven-foot-high windbreak fence, he said, "Guess your horse won't be jumping over that one." Or when he asked me to watch his horses while he was away, "If that old gelding don't move for two or three days, you might wanna call the vet." Or after a three-day grit storm, "Gee, don't the air smell fresh this morning?" Or when I managed to get my truck stuck in an irrigation ditch, "You probably don't want to just *leave* your outfit there for too long. Winter's coming . . . How 'bout I give you a little tug out?"

Doug didn't take it as far as the unintelligible mumbles of Ennis Del Mar, but he showed that a man just don't need to chatter much, unless he's got a good joke to tell or something important to say that nobody ain't heard a dozen times before.

There was a more contentious side to our relationship, though. One time in early May Doug and I were cleaning out the irrigation ditch. We were both down in the clayey bottom of the main stem, grubbing around in the mud and roots. Maybe it was the feel of the shovel or the weight of the sod, but the struggle—and it was the same old seasonal struggle: there's never *enough* water, and those downstream people in Hanksville have a prior right, so just when you need it most, in August, they get more than their share of it. And the damned spider-rooted sod always seems to grow, tangled up and hard to pull out, recalcitrant as children, or a bad dog—the struggle must have set him off.

"Them damned environmentals," he said, apropos of agriculture. "They're against *everything* human. Hell, where do you think *food* comes from? They sure don't grow it at the supermarket." He spat. "They have their way, we'd all be living in caves. Caves . . ."

I didn't look his way. Sometimes Doug would doff his sombrero and reveal the whitest forehead you've ever seen. His face was like some of the town-surrounding cliffs: red on the bottom, white above, and barren on top. I knew Doug was baiting me. We were a couple of bull elk in September. I studied the vegetation.

"Nature," he said. "I'll tell you something about nature . . . Hell, I'm just as much a lover of nature as any of them damned environmentals."

"Sure, Doug. No doubt about it."

People can take things personally if they want. The fact was the local water conservancy district, duped by a slick civil engineer from Spanish Fork, had big plans to build a cash-register dam one mile above town. This dam might well have provided *beaucoup* water to Doug and the four or five other ranchers on Poverty Flat, but the project had many problems, mainly economic and ecological, and I had been active in the dam's opposition, organizing the local anti-dam committee.

It was only natural for Doug to want to *improve* nature. That a reservoir full of water—impounded, stored, and used—would be an improvement could not have been more obvious. Also, you grow up in Hanksville as Doug had and doing virtually anything seems an improvement: shoveling sand from your driveway, gathering coal out on Factory Bench, hauling an old wreck off the place, dating someone who is not your cousin, making coffee. Improvements all.

I wanted to point out how the dam would end up costing way more than the dreamy predictions of the civil engineer, the engineer had deliberately played fast and loose with the facts, cash-register dams never pay for themselves, the reservoir basin would be an unsightly mudflat most of the year, constructing a power plant 800 feet from the border of a national park was a terrible idea, and so on, but I held my tongue. "You bet, Doug."

"And now them crooked politicians are starting to sound like environmentals, too. They sure couldn't make it any harder on us."

"No question about that. What does all that money go for anyway?"

The shovels went down easy enough, but the sod was heavy and entwined, hard on your back. We kept at it for another hour in silence except for grunting and occasional low curses. Maybe we taught each other a lesson.

—

Pretty as Doug Wells's pasture was, it proved easy living to just set outside and watch the cows and calves float along late in the day, legs half lost in timothy and wire grass. Or see how his Hereford-Angus cross range bull would call the ladies and kids over for a noontime lesson. Who cared about a few flies? Better cows than condos. Someday someone may carve up the pasture into a few choice ranchettes, but if you remember things the way they were before, you keep the image with you.

Sure, there was a flip side to it, and it came in late October and early November, or after calving time. Now, I'm fond of beef—broiled, grilled, basted, roasted, panfried, seared, barbequed—and find it hard to imagine any western American cow as holy. The selling and slaughter were what paid the bills. Still, certain times of year brought on the distraught cries of the mothers, and insofar as the little ones knew, they knew that the gambols of summer, the games of chase and buck, the taste of ditch water and good deep grass were over. The life of a cow leads only to Salina, and thence to the killing floor. April is a bad time not to have a calf at your side, and November is a deadly time to be a bullock.

In the end, though, it didn't pay for Doug. He had to sell the place to help pay medical bills for his stepdaughter. His duty demanded it, and he sold the ranch to a hobby cowboy, Larry, who rode a four-wheeler and didn't even own a decent horse. This new neighbor, aside from his fondness for the internal combustion engine (he once had his tractor, truck, four-wheeler, generator, air-compressor, and chainsaw all going at the same time) proved to be a gentleman, even if he wore a baseball cap and went to church every Sunday. He never gave me the slightest reason to soil his memory. Larry sold out four years later.

—

More recently, the pasture has been leased by Jones, a shithead from nearby Bicknell. Jennifer and my first meeting with Jones was a surprise—a surprise for him, since we showed up one weekend just as he was about to turn a couple of horses into our field. Once he saw us, he sped away. Jones made several other appearances while we were gone: he cut the fence, broke a gate, destroyed with a backhoe the stone bridge into the place that had stood for fifty years, let his cattle graze in the field *because the alfalfa was there and we weren't*. On another visit, when we met in the flesh, he attempted to deny all of the above to the very-pregnant Jennifer when the evidence was perfectly clear.

Jones then proceeded to explain how the problem was, actually, *you newcomers—people that come in here and try to tell us what to do with our land.* He said he just wanted to be a good neighbor, but he wasn't sure he'd be able to now. Jennifer begged his pardon and pointed out the land in question was *ours,* not *his.* She repeated the point, a bit louder. *Ours . . . not . . . yours . . .* An important distinction. She also explained that she was as much a Utahan as he was, and so was her husband. In addition, she mentioned that we paid property taxes—quite a bit of property taxes, actually—that benefited his children and the good people of Wayne County, and she didn't mind doing that, for the good of the community, because unlike Jones, to her the good of the community actually mattered. And that laws were laws, even in Wayne County.

Jennifer also amplified that she grew up in Cache Valley and knew quite a bit about agriculture—used to help her daddy irrigate the family farm in Mendon—and that the one thing you never did was cut someone's fence. Never. Never as in N-e-v-e-r.

Jones had cut our fence to let his stinking livestock in. We knew it perfectly well, and Jennifer pointed to the place where he had cut it, and we had fixed it, pointed to the dry turd piles, and repeated that she knew he had cut it, and when he denied cutting it and was about to call her a liar, I stepped in and said, *Don't you call my wife a liar, liar.* No, I told Jones that he was a couple-of-bad-words for hassling a pregnant woman as well as a purveyor of cow and horse poop, and I repeated he was a couple-of-bad-words fence cutter, and then I said that it would be a very good idea for him to leave and that presently, because he was a little several-bad-words-in-a-row coward. Because it takes me a little longer to get warmed up than Jennifer, to be entirely honest, at that point we were all pretty spun up.

Jennifer then shouted a variety of things about his honesty and manliness and penchant for busting up bridges and cutting fences.

He took his time walking away, shambling little greasy wing nut in coveralls. I hollered after him that I would call the sheriff to make sure it didn't happen again. I did. Oh, yes, Jones made a person nostalgic for the old days.

As did the parley with the deputy. Wasn't much he could do, of course, unless the cows or horses were actually on our property, but if they ever were on it again, then lock them in and call him, and he'd take care of it. But the word seemed to have traveled around, and Jones didn't graze his livestock at our place again.

He has since successfully run for the Wayne County Commission. His lease eventually ran out and was not renewed.

—

So, faced with the downhill trend of changes, I'd rather remember Doug in his hay days.

Years later, after I moved away and was living in Ogden, while driving on Highway 89, the freeway they built through his front yard in South Weber, I saw Doug Wells. I couldn't bring myself to stop. He had clearly aged, and I wanted to fix him in time, like a monarch butterfly, the kind that migrate through Good Water and feed only on milkweed, because there was so much of him that was both timeless and already vanishing.

Still, I imagine I see him occasionally, steering his old blue Ford tractor around the pasture, spreading fertilizer pellets in light-falling late-March snow.

Town Owl

1.

IT TAKES A VILLAGE, SURE, but it takes someone in that village, or rather up above in the trees of that village, watching and preying, to reinforce what is right and just. Not community standards, for the crowd is untruth and hell is other people, but an observer with scaly claws: tripartite holdovers from the days of the thunder lizards, tools used to cling to branches when the storms come rough and tumble, cat's paws for clutching prey.

The role of owl is mainly watching: ear tufts up, yellow eyes remarkably sensitive to detecting movement, head that can rotate around the compass, ears attuned to minutest vibration. With feathers mottled and blendy, a body down-garbed to last through winter's double shift.

A creature up above in the fir trees or cottonwoods, swooping in on silent sunset wings to alight, scrutinize, and speak. Alert, aware, and watching. Because when someone is watching, you flutter to somewhere you can defend.

Chorus with a memory. Keeper of the stories.

She had planted the trees. She had listened to the owls. When she went away the owls did too. Now they come in as guests and sense that something has changed.

An owl is a cat with wings. But there are too many cats and many are fed with spoons. Owls keep their strength by raising fewer young. An owlet learns to keep still enough to disappear in the crook of a limb, the hollow pecked by spotted birds. Songbirds will mob a hawk or eagle but leave owls alone. Leaves, bark, owlet, owl, camouflage.

Wind speed is higher off the ground. Owls learn the soft still shoals between the eddy and the stream.

If you learn the lay of the land you will find their clues and leavings: spots where owls hock up the bony parts of prey. These pellets show that seldom-seen birds have been here, roosted here, digested here, and left the things they could not use. In pellets is their evidence of preying. Mouse and vole, wood rat, gopher, shrew, ground squirrel, chipmunk. It's what's for dinner. Thence to return to a place that allows for looking down.

2

I wanted to learn about the early days and she wanted to tell me. Jet mused me with her memory. And with eighteen years in Grover and seventy in Good Water, she had a vast prey base. Dorthy Jenette "Jet" Hickman Smith was all about stories, anecdotes, proof to support her assertions that people were not always what they seemed.

With such a source, it was always good to pay a visit, even if a visit involved a considerable investment of time. Jet was not of the generation for which a visit is five minutes and see you later.

She was well into her eighties when I happened into her warren and had plenty of forage ground to cover. A visit consisted of a lengthy warm-up, hitting the stride with the freely associative monologue, always followed by refreshments. It was required to at least share a piece of cake. Beware if too much time passed between visits.

"What you been doin'? Why have you been neglectin' me?"

When she fixed you in her bottle-bottom glasses, you learned to beware the wrath of Jet Smith. There were people she liked or respected. Then there were people on whom she had some dirt. Anyone who knew her knew on which side to tread.

Jet despised a hypocrite above all others. Those who tried to cover their mistakes with leaves, who smiled and feigned righteousness while telling lies, whose deeds were pellets on rocks especially earned her ire.

It didn't matter if the relation was blood. In fact, of blood she knew more and farther. Her uncle Port Pectol was one she despised, for Uncle Port had appropriated stones, sandstone building blocks, from the construction of the Mormon meeting-house and used them to build the Wayne Umpire, his general store. Uncle Port, who was bishop and thus had access to a good many stones, had discovered some artifacts, some leather shields, he kept in a little museum in his store, and these artifacts contained temple symbols that he believed attested to the veracity of *The Book of Mormon*, although the shields were actually Navajo, from a few centuries after the mythic time of the Lamanites. To Jet, though, Uncle Port was the one who had stolen stones.

Another Jet despised was Jay Chestnut, long-serving mayor, who took credit for all Walt's work. Walt had installed the municipal water system, or most of it, not Jay, though Jay Chestnut crowed about it plenty.

She didn't spare her own brothers and sisters: Deseret, the golden boy; Laura, the wild one; Joe, the dirty alcoholic pup. And all of them were already gone, the only one left Madge, who seldom darkened Jet's door.

Then there was Vera Mulford, the town clerk and postmistress who, in cahoots with Jay Chestnut, had "tampered with the U.S. Mail. And that's a felony."

Within the category of hypocrites, people on whom Jet had some dirt, there tended to be a gender-based distinction: a man was generally referred to as "a no-good pup" while a woman was decried as "that dirty little huzzy." Often "rotten" wormed its way in as intensifier between the adjectives.

Jet was realistic about religion. A Mormon from her cradle, yet she had a livid feud with the current bishop, called him a dirty rotten pup and an awful poor dentist. She often went to worship with the Baptists, just across the street, who cultivated her. "The Lard don't care where you go to church just as long as you try to be a good person." And the Baptists saw it as a sort of coup to get Jet at service or socials.

Jet took an extra long time to walk across that street to and from the "gentile" church, and she spent a lot of time in the parking lot visiting, just in case one or more members of the Mormon ward happened to be driving by and would care to notice. The hippies, too, befriended her, and she them, as they were less judgmental.

With Jet there were people and there were geography and events, outlines to fill in and shade. What happened when the dances were held at Cozy Cove, the time Char Lee got in trouble for borrowing cattle he didn't actually own, the way the stuck-up people in Bicknell and Loa would treat folks from Good Water for having loose morals and living with the hippies, the one and only time Walt got drunk, what happened on the river bridge to Mrs. ——, how awful the folks up-county was and how they acted high and holy for no good reason, the things she remembered about her uncle Joseph Hickman—the one who drowned up to Fish Lake and gave a natural bridge in the national park the family name—the troubles with the Hiskeys over to Teasdale and the Colemans and the Forsyths, the prices at the Arm and Leg General Store, the weather, and the need for rain. She raked up huge piles of autumn lore.

To befriend and love an elderly person, though richly rewarding, involves the near notion of finitude. With contemporaries and friends, you hope for decades of companionship, a creel full of stories, and much in the fossil record to share. With a spouse is spun the spider web of years, with each new one a stronger skein until life without the other does not seem possible. To have children and that higher love entails clear evidence of your mortality as well as a hope that the better part of you might endure. But an audience with living history cannot feature interviews and anecdotes without number.

Many of us counseled against it, but Jet decided she was going to have that hip-replacement surgery, the one that she had put off all these years. Of course there were complications and a gift of infection from the hospital. They moved her to a rest home in Richfield to recover and made her share a room with another inmate. She hated it.

"If Wayne [her son] don't get me out of this place, I'm going to walk right out that front door and all the way to Good Water if I have to, and don't think I won't. I just can't stand it. You should try to live with *that* woman. She is crazy as a loon. She'll wake up right in the middle of the night and start talking to me, wants to get all kissie-kissie, says I was her dead husband John—whew!

"And the nurses are rude to me, and the food—I wouldn't feed it to my pup—and that no-good doctor, the one that made me so sick to begin with, he couldn't care less, too busy to visit." Her hands opened to the sky. "Well, I'll tell you this, every day I call up Wayne and Shirley and say, 'All right, you two, you come down here right now and get me out of this madhouse, or I'll walk all the way to Good Water if I have to. And don't think I won't!'"

3.

A ninety-one-year-old woman planting a garden.

The darned hip that had bothered her for fifty-three years replaced. The old folks' home in Richfield escaped. Reason enough to plant. But bushes? Bushes that would bear currants, black currants, but only three, four, five years down the line. There's a gesture to mortality; there's plans for the future.

To watch a ninety-one-year-old spindly woman plant a garden is a strange and wondrous thing.

It's the end of May. Dressed in a ratty overcoat and Walt's beat-up bowler, she leans on her cane and surveys her work. Soon she will drag the hose over and check the sprinkler head.

She has sown some things: sons and crops, a pretty good life between the ledges. When it rains her Red Mountain still shines like a thousand diamonds. Her gray eyes still flash like jet, the volcanic glass they nicknamed her for. Her body is still a body that can work. They sliced her open but did not succeed in getting rid of her. She is known in town and county, a fixture. She quilts because quilting is better than television, quilts for her great-grandchildren, quilts for the starving orphans in Romania.

Her columbines are growing, yellow and red. She waters them every day. *Have you ever smelled them up close?* The softest, sweetest perfume.

In the cool of the evening she tarries on the porch. The slurp of the canal, the rustle of the cottonwoods releasing fluff—*Don't it look just like snow this time of year, or sometimes like you're underwater?* It's tree love. The cool breezes sifted through the firs, the places the owls live. When it's too cold she'll move inside . . .

At ninety-one she still plants a garden. She leans on Walt's cane. She wears his worn-out coat and beat-up bowler.

She plants. She turns water on the garden.

She makes a calm day look windy.

Blue and Gray

I'M PITCHING HORSESHOES AGAINST A MAN FROM ALABAMA, a gentleman farmer and stock car aficionado, cousin-in-law of a friend. Marty is the type of fellow you'd want on your softball team: lanky, lithe, and strong. He could hit to place or swing for the fences and run like hell. He wears a seed cap and a ponytail. It's March. He tosses gray and I heave blue.

"Y'all have to irrigate around here?"

I tell him, you bet I do.

"How's that work?"

I point to the ditch at the upper, west end of the place, explain how I get four hours every twelve days, and that's enough if the grass has been eaten down.

"How much y'all pay for that water?"

"Fifteen bucks a year, more or less."

"And it comes from that one river back there?"

"It comes from that river. They bring it here in a canal that's about six miles long, dug by a Scotsman named Peaden, fifty years ago." I tell him to pay more attention to his tosses and stop trying to distract me. He says he's just getting warmed up.

"How many cuttings you get of that alfalfa?"

"Most years, three."

"Shoot," Marty says, "back home we get ten or twelve. All I ever did at my place was ride around on those damned swathers and balers. Got so sick of it I leased most of my land, got a job in a plant. Helluva lot easier work."

"Ten or twelve . . . That's four years here. And of course the only time it rains is in the summer when the hay is on the ground."

He nods, grimaces. Rain.

He's toying with me, I think. Sure he's spent hours, days, pitching shoes.

Marty lands a leaner, but it's vulnerable. On my second toss I knock it off the pole and take the lead.

"Y'all like playing defense?"

It's a rhetorical question. The greatest satisfaction in horseshoes comes from hurting your opponent. To score is good, true. To toss one that deprives him of points—to take away—is better. Best is the swing play: to take away points and also score. There's nothing finer.

Two turns later I toss a ringer. He tops it.

"Me too."

It's no great stretch to imagine Marty on a hot, misty morning at Vicksburg or Shiloh or Antietam or Andersonville. It must be the way he stands or his follow-through or the sound of the game. Marty's the type to kill a man and enjoy it—for a just cause. He's a handsome fellow with no scars, no tattoos, but you just feel it in your blood. Maybe it's the red dust of the pit or the occasional clang of metal, but as we walk between the pits, if I close my eyes,

I can almost hear the cannon and smell the rifle shot, taste the fear, see the violent bifurcation of life and limb, guts and blood, sense what will come in the buzzing of flies, the circling of buzzards, the solidness of stone walls, the silence of the dead.

Not that I have any ancestral resentment, mind you. My people sent no asthmatic clerk son from New London in defense of the Union, nor any Rebel son from Smyrna, Tennessee. No, my people didn't engage in the War between the States. They were busy being converted and crossing the plains, and, truth be told, they were pretty happy both sides were busy killing each other. It left them alone.

He might be thinking the same things about me.

"I'm playing horseshoes with this man from Utah, and he's probably a Mormon. He's got himself a pair of wives, keeps them well hidden, but tell you this, I've seen 'em, in the kitchen, baking peach pies, and they're ugly as sin. You know what they all say about those Utah Mormons and their horns. Well, let me tell you this . . . "

As I say, he's toying with me. It's dangerous to let the mind wander at sport. Even with the home court advantage, things are looking grim, my hopes fading in those clouds of red dust and clangs of metal.

He pokes two close ones in, and I guess for my part, the sun is in my eyes.

"Y'all didn't have to let me win like that just 'cause I'm a guest," he says. "Wanna play another?"

Burning Fields

UP AND DOWN THE VALLEY the earth sprouts plumes. Dark tails of ragweed and grass, overgrown ditches scorch into black lines between dried-out pastures. A whole summer's growth sent skyward in a minute by waves of flames fifteen feet high that scour the fields with crackling release. Igniting the old to make way for the new. An intentional scourge of sparks, smoke, soot, and speed. The flames spread like irrigation water soaking the fields.

You better pick a calm day. You better hold a shovel. You best enlist some buddies and leave the hose running by the buildings because once it gets started you might as well try to stop a blizzard.

What grew as mine can pass to yours—flames know no boundaries.

I saw it get away from Doug Wells one time. He'd been out there with his flamethrower, reenacting the assault on Mt. Suribachi, because nothing got to him like weeds, when the west wind sprang to life, and that fire moved so fast that by the time the fire department showed up, it was all over but smoking cow turds and a forty-acre shadow.

It has been duly proclaimed by elected authority that a special permit is required for any household burning, but a contrary motion is ratified *in flagrante delicto* by a hundred hands resting on the butt ends of shovels, watching as orange tendrils smoke, then blacken the idea of any parchment permission. Here's to you, County Commission, and up your nose for your trouble. Burn, baby, burn.

We give fire to the grass that once rustled like paper in wind, and each of us is entangled in the chance that low-banked smolders will flare to life and finally work themselves free.

When it's over, the fuel spent, the burned tufts poof to nothingness underfoot and the new year's growth shoots up free of competition, to rise for six months, grow and bud and flower, wave and dry and wither, and tempt us once again to burning these sere remnants of the summer sun.

Reliquary

The Moon looks like this after a long drought.

—Bill Holm, "Driving from Boulder to Hanksville, Utah"

Perched on its rusty parapet, Good Water surveys the vast tilted canyon-rific land. Sometimes the downward pull is too strong: you must go down. Down among the glorious snaky overdone, the white domes and buttresses and pinnacles, along the silty meandering Fremont River, through the Waterpocket Fold, spit out in the Old Gray badlands. Old Gray is Mancos Shale: lunar, barren, clay-rich, creepy. No place for cows, no place for people.

Eventually, as you roll east, two moony mesas rise up blue-gray, steep, and fluted. The first cottonwoods appear, then fields and scant houses of an oasis settlement. It is called Caineville. Caineville, Utah.

You might be tempted to keep right on going and maybe even move a little bit faster. You should. Oasis? The very idea of a settlement here seems out of place and oddly repellent.

Beyond the pale and never bustling, Caineville's population has eroded slowly and steadily since 1900 in the population dustbowl

that swept the rural West until it became "new." Forty people
live here today, one-third in one family. They lived until quite
recently without phones. For this reason alone the burg deserves
our admiration, but there's more. The town has no mayor, town
board, town meetings, planning, or zoning—and it shows splen-
didly. Anything goes. There are no town ordinances that might
infringe on personal freedom. Hell, there's practically not a town
at all.

From Caineville all roads radiate out like cracks from a windshield
chip and lead directly to trouble. Take the heartless Hartnet Draw,
for instance. Or better yet, don't. Stay on the main line for your
own moral safety, please.

Along the Hartnet it is actually possible to see the end of the
earth, *Finisterre*. And that will rock your world, Shirley. You
can drive toward it, too: up the axle-tweaking, kidney-testing,
chin-bruising Hartnet Draw. You can drop right off the edge out
there and never come back.

Stand at the South Desert overlook at the upper end of the
Hartnet and behold a pink-gray valley big enough to hold
Manhattan, with room to spare. Imagine Manhattan in there:
busy, roaring, fragrant, frenetic, a piggy bank. Blink and rub the
eyes . . . It was just a mirage. Maybe.

But note: halfway down the South Desert looms Jailhouse Rock,
the best-named feature in all of south-central Utah. A big ol' pink
Cadillac castle of a monolith: partly Tupelo, partly Gothic, and
partly Gaudí. Jailhouse Rock. I went to a party at the county jail
and didn't come back.

No matter which direction you travel from Caineville, the eyes
play tricks. Gray clay and blue sky blend into one and the same
hallucination. Miles pass with neither tree nor bush. Clouds take
on an inexplicable pink tint. Cows graze out there as a kind of
standing joke. Whatever you do, take plenty of water, matches,

firewood, scripture, a couple of cans of pintos, and never go out there at night. Never.

—

We knew an earnest graduate student from Utah State University, "Hartnet" John, who was attempting to study the impacts of cattle grazing on "vegetation" in the area and plotting different ways his bold research project would help him construct a gateway to a tenure-track job in the verdant groves of academe. And so Hartnet John consulted with his doctoral advisor, got himself a shiny new notebook, clipboard, and a dozen pens, set up transects in the field, and bought a cow from someone in Loa. Soon after he introduced the cow to the wide world of the Hartnet, the cow died. So did the next cow he bought, probably of a broken heart. And so on all summer long. One after another. The air must be bad out there.

—

With such dangerous and forlorn surroundings, then, it is best to stay close to town. Harshly beautiful, Caineville is the perfect place to take a walk in late October: with yellow cottonwoods rustling, the sky impossibly blue, no moisture in the mummified air, and a whole world of gray clay. Dora and I meet up at "Caineville" Jim's place and wait for Bob and Joanne.

I'm presently admiring Jim's wide-ranging selection of junk. He's got old counterculture vehicles: a VW bus, a couple of antique Subarus, an import truck up on piers, an old Power Wagon, as well as some defunct appliances, water-warped lumber, and busted furniture. Jim, he's got his eye on posterity. It's not what you do, it's what you leave behind.

To be accepted and flourish in Caineville a person needs a good junkyard. The handiest form of junk is automotive. By common consent, you won't be allowed into town without title to several useless vehicles, although in a bind, strings can be pulled so that someone's brother-in-law from Hanksville, twenty miles down the road, can be called on to part with a couple of wrecks. They've all got a few to spare. Just put those babies up on blocks and start collecting broken-down appliances for lawn ornaments. This is known as home improvement. Blessed is the junk, for it shall inherit the Earth.

Junk does not rust beneath these clear, dry skies. It does not move about on its own. It rests. It lingers. Weeds grow up beneath it. Small rodents call it home.

A few old cars and trucks scattered about the homestead, in addition to keeping down the dust and providing wildlife habitat, serve as a constant reminder that other tasks are more pressing than popping the hood of that old Plymouth. In this way, through the avoidance impulse, some work gets done: ditches dug and water tended, tamarisk whacked and cursed, livestock fed and gathered, and fields and ditch banks burned in springtime.

You see it all over the backwater West: collections of cars and appliances, manufactured relics in a kind of *Deliverance* cargo cult. Maybe there's some tiny value in the scrap metal or maybe people feel lonely without these paperweights of memory.

In the New England of Robert Frost, for instance, one pictures white or gray houses, meadows, ponds, orchards, and woodlots. Every place has a woodlot: a place for growing firewood. But notice in the weeds that the Volvos are rusting, slowly returning to earth. Here they don't quite rust, they just wait, not fading away.

In some ways Jim's a hippie because of his age and intolerance for the Man. In some ways, Jim's a tree hugger, too. A life-long union carpenter, he's had to scramble to make a living while living back of beyond. He's driven the school bus. He's built houses and traveled to build houses. He's gone to Loa when he needed a screw. He owns an Arabian gelding named Killer and a goat named Socrates, and he loves to sing and strum guitar. He'll do "Proud Mary" or "Lodi" at the drop of a nail gun.

Maybe Jim's junk lot is his memory shed. Hell, he loved those cars so much he just couldn't let go.

Sandy is Jim's girlfriend. She's from North Dakota, so no trees are no big issue for her. She has icy blue eyes, swollen starlet cheeks, and blond hair. She's smart, strong, and a science warrior: she works in the national park and used to work for the BLM, the Bureau of Land Management. She, too, will strum and sing and the slightest provocation.

Sandy leads the six of us across the river and toward our destination, the top of the South Mesa. She's been up there before and claims to remember the way. Sandy grows impatient, however, and we get lost.

Mancos Shale, more clay than shale, has the consistency of springtime slushy snow. It gives easily and provides good footing. When the going gets steep, you kick steps. Mancos Shale forms the baddest of the badlands, nude as pavement. We trudge clay gullies, arroyos, and gravelly fans, then scramble to the top of a blue-gray hill and see that we are still far from our goal.

Every few years, following an extremely wet March or April, these barren wastes exfoliate with trillions of tiny blooms, yellow and purple low-slung flowers that seem to grow out of nothing. They will color the badlands for a few weeks, but by the end of the summer, with the heat and endless wind, most sign of them will be gone.

Eventually Sandy relocates the right way and we trudge a mile-long flat. We then ascend a faint cow path that leads up the squaw skirts, to the foot of the cap rock. It's a head-scratcher to be sure: loose and steep and moonshiny. I'd just as soon trade my trusty Chesapeake Bay retriever, Joe Notom, for a good horse at times like these.

We pass through a rocky squeeze and gain the mesa top. Sandy has been told by ranchers that this is the only way to the top of the South Mesa, and you have to believe it.

On top at last, we are startled by the vast savannah. Sun-dried grasses cover the entire tabletop, rim rock to rim rock. You shouldn't call this "desert." No, this is a steppe—a high steppe—a place where tall grasses and low shrubs grow. And bizarre to boot: everything down there was barren and gray, but this sward would feed a bundle of cattle. Or it once did. This is classified as a relict grassland, a place that has not been grazed for a long period of time. The BLM has put a padlock on the gate of this pasture. No domesticated ungulates have grazed here for thirty-plus years. The mesa top acts as a giant seed factory, releasing the future on the prevailing.

Relict has a few further meanings. In addition to its botanical definition, it also connotes remnant, survivor, and widow. It's not a great stretch to see this place as a holy relict—a survivor of the way things used to be.

Bob and Joanne of Grover are fond of plants and begin to botanize furiously. Bob runs a landscape business and knows the common names of every grass and all the cacti. Joanne has a degree and impresses us with a smattering of Latin names. Dora joins in with the speculating. *Qu-est-ce que c'est?* As a reluctant naturalist, I'd rather not pin it down. We walk across the broad sweep of the mesa top east toward the Henry Mountains, spreading seeds and tossing appellations.

It's never enough to say, "My, this grass is delicate" or "Check this out: look at how thick or thin it grows" or even to try to ascertain its subtle gestalt. You've got to know the name. A name gives significance, meaning, importance, a category. Don't get me wrong, many of these names are fine, some are even poetic: needle-and-thread grass, shorty fescue, Indian rice grass, blue gramma, spiny hop sage, cliffrose, winterfat. We must name, we must bestow.

Names give order to chaos and articulate memory: give it a name and next time you see it you'll remember. Naming also celebrates abundance. "The grasses that grow on the mesa top" is insufficient. Divide and categorize, taxonimize. Do we not need a name before we can wonder?

"And what do you think, Joe?"

"*Woof*."

Joe doesn't really care. A bush is just a thing to piss on. One's as good as another.

We finally reach the eastern edge of the mesa top and gaze down upon the moon. The drainage below, named Sweetwater out of some perverse hope, is a worried blue-gray waste. Only along the spit of a long-dry stream is there any vegetation, a few lonesome cottonwoods. But for these scattered trees, between where we stand and the Henry Mountains, there is not one sprig of grass, not a bract of flower, not a leaf of grease brush. It is the most sublime vista I have ever seen.

Meanwhile, to the west, the scoliotic spine of the Waterpocket Fold juts up golden and reddish. To the north lies a limitless rise and fall of fortunately worthless country: Cedar Mountain, Cathedral Valley, Mussentuchit, Moroni Slopes, San Rafael—the castellated "Stone House Lands." A little overdone, all of this, too much, way too much. If a person came up here alone and really saw, really felt all this emptiness, marbles would be lost.

When did we come up here? Yesterday? This morning? Tomorrow? How did we get here? How on earth are we going to return?

We stand on a promontory of rusted stone, a promontory between moon and sky, surrounded by stunted trees burned black by a lightning strike. The wind of forever blows.

Stranger still is a house standing across the mesa top on a small rise. A house? Rub the eyes, blink, look again. It's still there. A stone house, a shelter, a crude and rustic hovel, all the way up here. We marvel as we walk toward it and wonder who built this thing.

It can't be Anasazi or Fremont Culture or Ancestral Puebloan; the roof design is a dead giveaway. We figure it was built by sheep-herders or cattlemen. There's plenty of building material around: rock to use to make shelter from the storms. A story and a half of buff-brown stones wrested from the ridge and dry set. Inside we find planks that must have been brought up on the backs of beasts of burden. Still, it seems almost a useless extravagance. The cool seasons, spring and fall, and some winters would have been graz-ing times up here, times when the water pockets were full. This house would probably be too far from the settlement to go up and down every day, but given that there is just one way up or down, why would anyone need to stay up here and watch over the critters when a good gate would suffice?

Maybe it served as some kind of clubhouse for games of chance, moonshine, or rituals involving incense and oils, a refuge for meetings of the high priests, for Freemasonry, for Druids (a little short on trees), for the laying on of hands. At the very least it might have formed a fine excuse for the men of Caineville to get away from hearth and home. Or to bring the hearth and home along. Maybe this was a little lovin' shack beneath the rampage of stars.

The ladies . . . Maybe the men stayed home and the women ran riot. Empowerment for the sisterhood. Refuge for the better halves. Perhaps there was a secret matriarchy thing going on up here, a Wicca, a coven, a Relief Society gathering. But yikes, it's a story and a half.

Maybe the Mormon settlers had to put a roof on it. As much of it as there is, to sleep beneath this nail bed of stars was simply too much.

Because really that's where religion starts. First you give a name to the Other—sky, stars, grasses, mesa top—and then you won-der. You stand outside in high country with fragrant arrowy pines and look up into the night-iced sky and wonder—why am I here?

At least in the mountains you feel yourself surrounded and not the tallest thing around. Then come to Caineville Mesa and you may leave a snail or a god. Churches, roofs, sheds, junk lots all confine and control and give a meaning to our suffering, a protective way to deal with it. A dome overhead painted with saints and gods that look like us. Ancestors on a sandstone wall. A roof on the house on the mesa top.

Packrats have taken over the place in the meantime. Some floor planks have been used for kindling. The roof now opens to the sky.

Surely this dwelling is haunted, has to be. And the winds that race across the mesa top, the whisper of the swaying grasses, the bleat of the nighthawk, the groan of distant thunder, the white noise of all this emptiness—here's a place to behold Deity.

We talk of our fancy to send a weekend or a week up here, a week cast away on a tawny island in the sky, in a stone house full of holes and rats and the ghosts of men and their long-dead sheep and cattle. We picture night: the savannah would stretch bone-white in the moonlight while spirits passed over like a murmuration of grackles.

Strolling north, Dora finds a chert spear point amid the sand and gramma. Mormon sheepherders were evidently not the first people to tread this mesa top. We speculate whether the aboriginal inhabitants lit fires to drive game, whether they ambushed deer or desert bighorns at the crest of the only way up, what they saw when they looked across the eastern gulf. Would it have seemed moony? Did they name the grasses? Where were the water pockets and springs? Were they the ones who put all this juju here?

At the gateway again, we pause, rest, and watch fading light gild Old Gray. We then rip down the squaw skirts and cross the void of badlands on sun-baked clay that crunches underfoot.

Crossing the river in near dark, we are surprised at how warm the water is, much warmer now than in the morning. It's a flow reminiscent of springtime Alpine waterfalls that are a trickle at daybreak, melt to life in the afternoon, and roar into the night. In crossing water we leave the netherworld for the real world. Well, not quite. The real world doesn't intrude here.

Great Jove, we are hungry! Jim fries up a mess of vegetables and kielbasa. We swill cheap, tepid beer and give thanks for our pilgrimage to the mountain to see the burning bush. Parishioners, celebrants, supplicants, friends forever. We eat with our fingers. The vegetables and sausages taste heavenly.

H_2O

USE IT OR LOSE IT

NOTHING IS MORE IMPORTANT TO A DRY LANDS RANCHER than water. Nothing could be more frustrating than to witness what little water there is go unused. Good, fresh, nutrient-rich, high-mountain water flowing by, untouched, downstream. Not flowing in ditches and not pressurized in pipes. Heading downstream because it is already appropriated and the water right belongs to someone else. Or flowing downstream because of the alleged needs of some useless creature no one ever heard of that requires certain in-stream flows, creatures such as the flannel-mouth sucker or the bony-tailed chub or the Colorado pike minnow. Or, to extend it a little, the spotted owl or northern goshawk or reintroduced Canadian wolves: creatures used by the toadstool worshippers to destroy the rancher's way of life. Or because of drought, and there's not much that can be done about drought except to tend and grow resentment. Climate change, my eye.

But speaking of facts, certain historical truths regarding water can't be ignored, two in particular: water rights have always been first come, first served—or first stolen—and even given that, water tends to flow toward money, political power, and population. Wayne County is short on all of these.

The unexploited water in the Fremont River, for instance, flows eventually to California. It's good water turning bad. Nothing is worse than California, except perhaps Mexico. California lurks somewhere downstream at the end of the journey. Everything past Glen Canyon Dam is California. California—reaching out to all of us. California—preaching on the Golden Shore.

People in Wayne County are like Tantalus in the myth—the water they need is there, pooled, but out of reach. It can't be used to grow alfalfa to feed cattle, and in the high-elevation Interior West, hay and cattle are pretty much the only crops that are possible. Although the water's source may be the backyard high country, much of the water has already been spoken for and belongs to someone else.

Good Water was settled in 1888 or 1890 and was canal-less for decades. Certainly there were some downstream users then, but the big push for downstream use—and the big steal—came after the Colorado River Compact of 1922 and the explosive growth of Los Angeles, Phoenix, and Las Vegas.

The Fremont River becomes the Dirty Devil at Hanksville and eventually flows into Lake Powell. Much of it evaporates in that reservoir or in Lake Mead. Much of it is used in downstream cities and farms. Very little Fremont River water ever reaches Cali; most years none reaches Mexico. This fact ought to cheer up small-time ranchers. But facts prove less than relevant when we're talking about water in the West. The water begins its journey here. It falls as snow and melts. It's born here, dammit. It ought to be used here too, dam it.

Regarding the Colorado River, of which the Fremont is a tributary, Utah is an Upper Basin state, which is to say it is the source of the water. But when it comes to allocation or water rights, Utah gets screwed. There are complicated reasons for this. The Colorado River is overallocated, which means that there are more claims for the water than there is actually water in the river. In fact, there is a water deficit of several million acre-feet per year.

Placed side by side, the Upper and Lower Basins have half-empty glasses, but both basins like to pretend that both glasses are full. Overallocation is like government deficit spending: it's a fact that can be ignored for a finite period of time. Someday, though, there will be a reckoning . . .

Upper Basin states possess what are known as "reserve" rights, but the reserve rights can only be "redeemed" by developing water—say, by impounding it in a storage reservoir. In the spirit of overallocation, the Wayne County Water Conservancy District (WCWCD), as is the case with countless rural water districts in the Interior West, has a reserve water right to 55,000 acre-feet annually, *provided* it can store the water and put it to use.

The reserve right: catch it, store it, use it or lose it.

This proviso is the heart of this story.

The best way to store water aboveground is in a reservoir. A reservoir is a practical concept: the water just sits in it, stored, to be used as needed. Spring runoff can be carried over for three or four months and then be released when it is most needed for late-season irrigation. The challenging part is to build the dam that will hold the water. To build a dam is quite expensive and brings with it a host of annoying environmental considerations.

In the 1930s America built dams that were the envy of the world. The dam-building binge continued until well into the 1960s. By the 1970s, though, people such as Jimmy Carter noticed that federal dam building was a boondoggle, a tremendous waste of taxpayer money, the many benefiting the few.

At the same time, the environmental movement was burgeoning. One article of faith, based on the writings of Wallace Stegner, David Brower, Edward Abbey, Ann Zwinger, and many others, is that dams are one of the worst things that can be done to a wild river. To some extent science had come to the service of dam haters as native species now received required habitat protection under the Endangered Species Act. Moreover, in 1976, Idaho's Teton Dam failed, causing widespread destruction and some deaths, and this sent ripples through the governustrial complex. The era of dam building was over.

But not in Wayne County.

It came to pass that a very small reservoir and a very large dam were proposed to be built one mile upstream from Good Water.

Dams and reservoirs do two other things in addition to storing irrigation water. They provide recreation, and they can be used to generate electricity. Many Wayne County residents loved the idea of motorized recreation in their backyards—jet skis and powerboats and boat fishing. A pocket-sized red rock reservoir playground would certainly be a boost to tourism as well as good clean fun.

Furthermore, Wayne residents were familiar with the benefits of clean, cheap hydropower. Fully one-half of the electricity of the local electrical cooperative came from hydropower sources: most from Glen Canyon Dam and some from a small cogeneration facility near Boulder. And when it came to hydropower, Wayne County residents observed one thing: it generated no air pollution. When the environmentalists grumbled about water quality and ecological damage, most Wayneites smiled and thought that they obviously wanted it both ways: if you don't like dams, then what's the alternative? Coal-fired plants and nuclear, both of which seemed demonstrably worse. Hydro is clean. *What, do you want to live in a cave?*

And so the wet dream surged on, the dream to build a modest reservoir, only three or four miles in length, but a reservoir that would provide each of the following in abundance: storage for the 55,000 acre-foot reserve water right, way more water for irrigation and less to California, and bubbly for recreation. In addition, this dam would impound and carry over preservation of the rural way of life, create countless jobs—hundreds, if not thousands—and give a hat tip to heritage, a warm feeling of progress based on a triumph over nature by exercising human control. Furthermore, the dam would keep the children of Wayne County from fleeing to the Wasatch Front at their first opportunity.

How could this be possible?

The answer was given by a slick civil engineer from Spanish Fork, Utah, named Murdoch. The Wayne County Water Conservancy District would construct what is known as a cash-register dam. The dam would be equipped with electrical generating capacity. The electrical energy generated would be sold. The revenue generated by the sale of electricity would be used to pay for the loan to build the dam as well as to pay to pump the water uphill to irrigate the alfalfa fields of Rabbit Valley. And the best part of all this was that it wouldn't cost a penny.

Murdoch convinced his patrons, who were well-meaning if somewhat credulous people, people who believed in miracles and hated outsiders, that the dam would magically pay for itself in twenty years, and the rest—all that extra water—would be gravy.

From the outset the idea was delusive and outdated. It violated a tenet of John Wesley Powell's nineteenth-century observations that irrigation reservoirs should be built high in the mountains, near the source of the water, in steep canyons, on tributary rather than main streams, and above the fields that would be irrigated. Gravity should do the work from there.

In the past rural farmers looked to other taxpayers, especially those who lived in places such as Michigan, Florida, Illinois,

Tennessee, New York, California, and West Virginia to finance their dams. But by the 1980s that pool of money had dried up. This is why Murdoch hatched a plan that had the added benefit of costing nothing at all.

The year was 1989, however, and things were not nearly so simple.

Arrangements for Murdoch's cash-register dam were in early full swing when I came to town. Plans had been drawn up and permits were about to be filed for. Obviously a dam in scenic southern Utah would attract the attention of the environmental community, but a couple of features of Murdoch's plan sent up lookie-heres spurting like geysers.

In order to generate electricity there needs to be sufficient water pressure within the dam, as is the case with the giant concrete ones such as Glen Canyon or Hoover or Grand Coulee, to turn turbines. In concrete dams the intake valves make a natural whirlpool, water is sucked down through the dam at enormous pressure to turn turbines, and the water is then spewed out into prime trout habitat below.

Alternatively, in the case of earthen-fill dams, such as the Good Water one, water needs to flow downhill several hundred feet in pipes in order to get enough hey-now to spin the turbines. Topography worked against Murdoch from the outset. The dam site was in the middle of a relatively flat little valley. In order to get a 700-foot drop, reservoir water would have to be moved in canals several miles to the Fremont Gorge, where the river begins its precipitous drop to Fruita. Within the Fremont Gorge the water would be forced into pipes, called penstocks, and sent downhill to turn turbines at the bottom.

The magical plan ran into two delicate issues here. Moving the water in costly canals would require de-watering the Fremont River, making it no longer a river for several miles. De-watering streams is a process that creates numerous ecological impacts and is generally unpopular with government land-management agencies. Worse, perhaps, was that the planned power plant just happened to be located 800 feet west of the boundary of Capitol Reef National Park.

The Park Service would have to pay attention to this, which created a real pickle for the park superintendent, a local boy named Marty Ott, who sought nothing more than accommodation to the interests of the local populace. Roadless Fremont Gorge was in fact being considered for potential wilderness designation. A power plant, roads, transmission lines, penstocks, and all that would have an impact so significant it could not be ignored. Building a dam and de-watering the river would also alter the Fremont River, the most significant watercourse in Capitol Reef National Park. The Park Service expressed guarded concern with the consequences the proposed dam would have on water quality: increased salinity, higher PH, reduced oxygen content, changes in temperature, and so on, while Ott worked to assuage the concerns of the locals.

While Murdoch schemed and the WCWCD dreamed, outsiders began to take notice.

Dam hating by environmentalists goes back to the battle for Dinosaur in the 1950s. Two of the green holy books, *Desert Solitaire* and *The Monkey Wrench Gang* by Edward Abbey, detail the reasons to be a detester of dams. Some of this line of argument is aesthetic and cultural, which is to say subjective. Another book had just come out, though, that was more grounded in fact, science, and truth: Marc Reisner's *Cadillac Desert*. *Cadillac Desert* appeared in 1986 and wrote the epitaph for federal dam building in the West.

Cadillac Desert demonstrates by facts and evidence the history of reclamation in the West: what had started as a legitimate idea had grown into a self-serving hydra of agencies and private industry. You can hate dams all you want, but this backstory is actually more important and provides more ammunition.

Few, if any, in Wayne County had heard of, much less read, *Cadillac Desert.*

We had.

We were Southey Swede, who owned Capitol Reef Inn; Jack Spence, a retired chemistry professor; and Dora and I. We formed the core of the local opposition group.

We didn't bother with a name, figuring that we'd just be known as those damn anti-dam people. Part of our problem with the dam was personal: we didn't really want the riffraff that the project would attract—not in the construction phase—and Good Water had no infrastructure whatsoever to deal with it, or with the motor-happy petro-based recreationalists who would come later. Both of these arguments were a little too precious to hold much water, though. Partly it was aesthetic. Dams tend to be a little intrusive, particularly a nearly mile-wide dam a mile upstream from town. Partly it was ecological. A power plant next to a national park and de-watering a river that flowed through one could easily be considered insane. We called meetings to be held at Southey's inn.

At the first invitation-only meeting, several Park Service people showed up on the sly, and to spy, as did a few interested citizens, maybe two dozen people. We brainstormed different ways to try to stop the dam. We sensed we had to go beyond Wayne County, since the calculus would be drawn as we dam bad, they dam good.

We couldn't argue with the dam proponents on cultural grounds (that dams were not good things)—that was a no-winner. We knew our best strategy was to use science within the system, to examine all the documents—Murdoch's plans, the EIS (environmental impact statement) scoping statements, and the FERC (Federal Energy Regulatory Commission) applications—to find the loopholes. We also sensed that the project's Achilles' heel was economic, namely, that it made no economic sense.

From the outset we faced opposition to our opposition. I was not invited back to my seasonal job with the Park Service because of my wintertime work on the anti-dam committee. Marty Ott, as I've said, wanted no trouble with the locals. He didn't need some peon seasonal employee making trouble. He was on a knife edge, though. He had to protect the resources of his park, knew that the dam would be an ecological problem and public relations nightmare, but wanted to work in secret to oppose it. The last thing he wanted was several of his employees yakking it up in public in opposition. Many Park Service people supported our side, but they all lived in Fruita, in Park Service housing called the Fish Bowl, rife with spying and informants, and the Parkies had few ties in Wayne County but lots of ties to the paycheck.

We received threats from our fellow citizens. Sometimes one sensed a spirit of something less than love in the air. We also received quite a bit of unsolicited advice, mainly along the lines of cease and desist. Our opposition was generally a bafflement, for it was impossible to understand how we could oppose a project that would cost nothing, promote progress, and keep the kids in the county. Southey's café was on the do-not-visit list for the locals, but it didn't matter. Southey knew that his bread and butter were tourists from Europe making the parks circuit in rental cars.

Jack Spence had no economic ties to the community, and because he had been fighting environmental battles for four decades, he was not bluffed by any of the bluster. He lived quite a distance from town, however, on some isolated acreage, and his safety would never be guaranteed by the law enforcement officers of Wayne County. But Jack owned several guns.

Over many cups of coffee we plotted. We fulminated and stamped our feet. Jack Spence insisted that the science was bad but the real weakness was money. "Who's gonna pay for it?" he'd say. "Who's got that kind of money around here?"

Murdoch had pulled the $20 million figure out of the dark recesses of his overburden. Through fuzzy math he was able to put forward the premise that the sale of electricity would generate $1 million a year. One times twenty equals twenty. Presto, the project would pay for itself in twenty years. The math was funny, sure. And it also didn't even come close to adding up.

Money generally does not grow on trees, and borrowing money was not exactly free in 1989. A loan at 5 percent for twenty years, for example, requires a monthly payment of $131,991.15, which adds up to $1,583,893.80 a year, which is a sum significantly larger than 1 million, and paid out over twenty years, 20 million actually becomes 30 million.

Moreover, using the project's planning documents, we calculated that at an extremely low rate of $15 an hour (in nonunion Utah in 1990), the labor costs alone (based on man-hours estimates of the planning documents) would be well over $15 million. This said nothing of the cost of land acquisition (the WCWCD did not own any of the land upon which the dam would be built or the water that would be impounded; it would have to be bought or taken by eminent domain). Not to mention the material for the dam, or constructing the canals, penstocks, transmission lines, new roads to the power plant, and the power plant itself. Let's not leave out the exhaustive documentation necessary to get a federal license, or the environmental impact statement or environmental analysis. Nor did any of this include the mighty pumps that would push water back uphill to irrigate fields located at 7,000 feet above the sea and 400 feet higher than the dam (the dam would actually be located below most of what little arable land existed in Wayne County). No, we calculated that even in the rosiest scenario, the dam would cost somewhere between $60 and $80 million, if WCWCD were extremely lucky. And paying back $80 million at 5 percent over twenty years would require over $500,000 a month, $6.3 million a year, figures sure to lead to exceptionally steep rates for clean electricity. And $80 million would grow to $130 million.

Meanwhile, the WCWCD circled its wagons. When faced with outsider troublemakers in their midst, people who were not from *here*, who were prepared to tell *us* what do to with *our* land, well, it was an old story and an old reaction. WCWCD took on its own agitprop. It signed a contract with the local electrical cooperative ensuring that there would be a buyer for the power (even at ten or twenty or thirty times the cost of the 2¢ per kilowatt hour of Glen Canyon power.) The matter was discussed in testimony meeting. Us against them is a very potent idea in southern Utah. A century of history reinforced it until it was far beyond an article of faith; it was a matter of vital fluid. Water is blood to a desert cowboy.

Where exactly would the $20 (or $80) million come from? Wayne County was among the poorest counties in Utah and it boasted just over 2,400 inhabitants. Those 2,400 people weren't going to cough up the money; they didn't have none. Hell, in those days you could sell all the private land in the county and you'd be hard pressed to scare up $20 million.

In the old days, the federal government would have been called upon, but in 1990 the federal government was out of the dam-building business. Why would any government fund a project to benefit a few part-time ranchers whose land was over 7,000 feet high? The state government, too, was then headed by Governor Michael O. Leavitt, who had Wayne County roots. At the time, however, Wayne County was not in Leavitt's best graces. This was due to some adverse publicity about whirling disease first discovered at one of the family's fish hatcheries in

Wayne County, perhaps planted by disgruntled Wayneites. Love for the Leavitts was also diminished by the family propensity to acquire distressed Wayne County acreage at fire-sale prices. So the guv wasn't likely to back the project. The only possible source for the funds would be bonding.

What bank on earth would use the collateral of 2,400 souls and no economy for a $20 (or $80) million loan? Interest rates would be high and the terms punishing. Throw out the fuzzy math and it was easy to see that the project would never pay for itself. The future of Wayne County would be mortgaged: the Good Water dam would leak red ink in perpetuity.

Murdoch's plans grew more complicated and grandiose with each revision, until the final iteration of the dam would be four-fifths of a mile across—about the length of the Grand Coulee Dam, though not as massive.

Public meetings were held. We, the damn anti-dam people, tried to confine our comments to economics. I held up a placard with the man-hours calculation, showing that it would easily cost over $20 million in labor fees alone. Murdoch blithely responded that that's not the way you calculate costs. How do you calculate costs, Mr. Murdoch, and how much will this cost? What about the land acquisition, material, power plant, canals, EIS, roads, licensing fees, and so on? He answered, you guessed it, $20 million, son. Where is this free money going to come from? What if it costs several times that much? Murdoch held fast to his bogus calculator. The crowd was assured by his talk. He said it would cost $20 million, you jerk.

Southey reiterated the economics of bonding, of loans, of cost overruns, of the pork barrel, of lawsuits, of federal licensing fees, and was met with hostile stares and some gnashing of teeth.

Most of the others in our anti-dam group were unwilling or unable to speak. Not that it would have done any good anyway. Facts had little importance.

Just to show that the good people of Wayne County were behind the project, in November 1990 a public referendum was attached to the ballot. The voters were asked whether or not they supported the efforts of WCWCD to continue to pursue this water development project. The results: 97 percent of those who cast ballots voted with the WCWCD. We were not surprised or completely disheartened. We felt we had a small victory with 3 percent against the dam, pretty good results at the time.

We knew that we would have to take the fight elsewhere.

We held a big confab in Salt Lake City. Representatives from the Southern Utah Wilderness Alliance, the Sierra Club, the Sierra Club Legal Defense Fund, the Wilderness Society, the Utah Wilderness Association, and the National Parks Conservation Association attended. We discussed the make-believe economics of the plan, how the Wayneites were being duped by Murdoch and WCWCD.

We were told by the representatives of the big environmental groups that it was a good thing that we had a local group. The only way to stop this sort of project, once it got beyond a certain point, was to go to court and sue on our behalf. That was certainly something to look forward to. We were thanked for our efforts and told to be careful down there in Wayne County. Lock your doors; don't stand by windows; keep your meetings quiet.

The environmental groups would certainly have sued on our behalf. Bad economics, significant environmental impacts, and fuzzy math didn't have the same cachet in 1990–1991 as they might have forty or sixty years earlier. We recognized that the plan was outdated and impractical. But Murdoch kept getting fees, the project kept getting grander, WCWCD still had that undammed water right.

So why is there no dam today on the Fremont River one mile upstream from Good Water?

A quiet conspiracy of opposition killed the harebrained scheme. FERC had a potpourri of sticky questions about the application. The National Park Service whispered reservations about the project when no Wayneians were listening. Governor Mike Leavitt wouldn't publicly support it. The state Division of Wildlife Resources, purged of troublemakers in the whirling disease vendetta, expressed guarded concerns. Environmental groups saw this proposal as a test case, and one they could take to the courts and win. Litigation worked, and here was a situation where the combined force of Utah's enviros could hardly lose. There was local opposition, some well connected, and the local opposition was active into the wider world. We did our part. The Wayne County Water Conservancy District didn't really have the political clout to line up supporters from beyond its borders. Where the heck was Wayne County, anyway?

Murdoch, satisfied with his ten years of fees, slipped out the back door when no one was looking.

Like a phoenix, however, the project has risen from the ashes. You can't entirely kill a really bad idea—it's just not human nature. No, the Wayne County Water Conservancy District has a new plan. It's still in the early stages of development, but now they want to dam the Fremont River on the other side of the national park, a location of significantly less environmental impact. The project will be designed to give a handful of farmers in Caineville and Hanksville more river water to grow more alfalfa and larger melons, to blossom up some of that fine, fine farmland, alkali flats, and sand dunes.

If WCWCD can't actually develop the water and secure the direct water rights, it can lease them to other entities. For instance, the proposed nuclear plant at Green River, Utah, the Blue Castle in the Sand, is going to need a tremendous amount of water to operate, more than 55,000 acre-feet, certainly, but Wayne County might as well get in on that action. If Wayne doesn't lease the water rights to Blue Castle, someone else will. Maybe lease the water for a few years, bank the proceeds, and then start again on a dam.

So the rainbow-after-rain dream to use 55,000 acre-feet of good, fresh, nutrient-rich, high-mountain water will always be here, even if it seems dormant as a cicada.

Water still goes by unused, untouched, untroubled, flowing downhill but not to the sea.

Part Two

Joe's Mesa

By the time we got to Good Water, the hippies were two or three dozen strong. Dora and I became part of the clan. Although at least a decade younger than most of them, we were still part of the same generation, albeit the tail end. Eschewing careerism and wanting to do it our own way, too, we were wide-lapelled children of the '60s and '70s.

Some of the hippies had traveled to Southeast Asia. Some had worked out deferments. They had all carried placards at one time or another. Seeing that the war and all that contributed to it was FUBAR, the Good Water hippies drifted down to their little edge community and stuck. Many kept their hair long and flower-strewn in time of need. At one time nearly every young person in town was allied with the clan, even the rednecks.

I knew I had arrived when one fine day in March I was invited to go up Joe's Mesa with the hippie triumvirate: Bird, Owens, and Manny. Joe's Mesa was named for Joe Hickman, Jet Smith's brother, a derring-do cowboy and notorious drunk. That he actually took cattle up the beer and skittles funhouse route to the mesa top remained an enduring marvel: the gouges of cattle hooves in red-orange sandstone could still be seen on the steep sections. The hippies adopted Joe into the clan as a cinch belt to the past, or rather he adopted them, as there was often a meeting in the wee hours when Joe was out on a spree and would stop by Manny's or Bird's and demand entrance and entertainment. Cowboy and hippie could join together on the edge for cross-pollination.

Owens and Bird had known each other since they were kids in the same private schools in Phoenix. Owens had inherited the Arm and Leg General Store from his daddy and became active in the volunteer fire department and civic affairs. Owens had a roster of enemies. He and Effie Dougan, who owned the Bridle N Bit Bar, had once come to slaps during a town council meeting over water hookups.

Bird had inherited enough from his folks that he didn't need to work, which was good, as work was not his strength. No, his métier was idleness. His other calling was to constantly question Manny's greatness. Another of Bird's vocations was his ability to maintain composure even when he was out to lunch. He wasn't a macho guy who boasted of how he held his liquor and stuff, but Bird could be on everything but roller skates and never really show it. I found it something to admire and emulate. He mentored me on many a late-night soiree. I spent many a glittering hour at Casa Bird, where good times were nearly always possible. Bird was my best friend in town. His lady, Anna, was like a sister.

Manny Lee had grown up in the Garden State and had made it west to pack the trail for his kid sister Anna, who eventually followed Manny and cohabitated with Bird. Manny's talents were numerous, especially in carpentry, design, jewelry, and Jack Daniels, and his preeminence was acknowledged by everyone except Bird.

Naturally it took plenty of time to get the party together. First there was Bird of the Thousand Indecisions: one bagel or two, which sweater, which shoes, which shades, how many doobies, why bring a first-aid kit, how many packs of smokes, which backpack, what to drink? To propose a hike with Bird meant waiting on Bird. Manny and Owens, too, had their own demerits vis-à-vis hiking.

Owens had indulged vices such as smoking and drinking heavily for years. He had had a major cardiac event the year before and nearly croaked. Such a generally mellow hike might be good therapy for Owens. Still, we all feared Owens would seize up somewhere along the way, turn white faced, grab his roaring chest, and keel. The possibility of cardiac arrest kept things interesting. Might as well try it, though. There were far worse places for Brother to go down.

Manny, too, was suffering from major heart problems. He had recently lost his wife, Marielle, to brain cancer. Marielle was a lovely person, teacher, painter, horsewoman, feisty princess from Westchester. But Marielle was tracks lost in the snow. We all missed her and remembered the horror of her leaving.

With all that, I didn't consider our prospects very good.

The trail up to the first ledge led through the upper half of the Chinle formation, clay slopes interspersed with more solid conglomerate layers and plenty of orange talus sprinkled down from the Wingate cliffs above. The old cattle trail, though, was easy to follow, and this first hill ought to have been surmounted in about ten minutes. There was no reason to dawdle, no marvelous place to stop and wonder. The strategy should have been just to get it over with and get where things leveled out and got better.

But no, not for Team Slowpoke. Bird, Owens, and Manny took half an hour just to get up the measly hill. I was up above on the rim rock, pacing, wondering how it could possibly take so long. I watched them down below taking rest stops. I went back down and said, "Hey, man, are we going to hike today or just diddle around and pet our bunions?"

No response. I herded them up the hill. Following another long rest stop, we finally took to the ledge, passing beneath brassy Wingate cliffs.

In the Swiss system—slow and steady—this flat mile or two would be dispatched in an easy plod. The rabbit hiker would blast ahead, stopping three times to catch her breath and look around before taking off again, each step stretching righteous resentment. A Larry-like-the-Wind wouldn't stop until reaching Red Gully. Not these Good Water hippies, though. One hundred yards was good progress. Satisfied with the quota, it would be time to sit down on a rock, have a smoke, take a few pulls of the vodka and something, talk-about-it, then saunter another heaping 100 yards. In the sauntering process, at least we weren't going to miss the view.

Manny and Bird looked like they could be brothers: tall, bearded, and blond. They fought like brothers, too. Manny thought Bird wasn't good enough for Anna Lee, of course, but never actually expressed it. All Manny said when Bird wasn't around was that he was a moron, as well as a complete idiot, and vice versa. Owens was blond, too, but thinning.

Owens loved to keep up to date on all things good and watery. He was a fixture behind the counter at the Arm and Leg, with droopy walrus mustache and rheumy terrapin eyes, yakking it up behind clouds of smoke, about the dam, about that such-and-such Effie Dougan, about the German tourists, about the real-estate lady, about the fire department budget, about the weather, about the oh-my-goodness water hookups at the Rimrock, at the Egyptian, how there was no way the town can hook up those people (his competitors) with city water. *It'll all run out and we'll be left high and dry.*

It was going to take us two hours to cross that first ledge.

Meanwhile, there rested and wheezed Owens and his fucked-up ticker. His face was turning an intriguing shade of sky blue. All this partying strained his raisin, but he kept right at it. He avoided the herbal supplement, naturally, being a businessman, and knowing how it messed up the columnar entries of his mind, and also because Owens was refinding his ancestral home within the GOP. Not all hippies are liberals.

No, there are two classes of the reactionary hippies. The more common variety is the rednecked hippie, common in rural regions. Redneck hippies, to speak broadly, like guns, carrying guns, huntin' with guns, big beautiful trucks, working in mines, living in trailers, cutting their own firewood, growing their own, and especially not being told what to do by the Man—it's the Libertarian / Don't Piss on My Gate school of counterculture. And really quite a lot of fun it is, too.

People like Owens, on the other hand, who were not working class in origin, and who held placards in college and worked out deferments, had given over their flowers and beads to the altar of the almighty *denaro*. A hippie businessman or woman is a kind of deformed wonder to behold. Just as the best sinners go on to make the best saints, so too Owens and his damaged blood pump taught that peace and love only go so far.

His prices were sky high. How many times had I heard him say, "Well, you know, I'm trying to keep the prices down, but hell, it costs so much in transportation just to get stuff here . . . You seen the price of gas lately?"

This was all baloney, of course, because his bread and butter were tourists, European tourists, who thought $70 for a bag of groceries is "not so bad for holiday in Amerika."

This is the way he explained global trade: "Hell, the Krauts are killing us economically anyway, their currency is way stronger, and that's why they keep coming . . . in droves."

I had my college German going on just then, as well as experience in tourism, and softly mocked my shower-challenged Teutonic friends.

"Have you informations in Cherman?"

"Have you a mop of Ooh-Tah? Dis state, OOOOOh-Tah?"

Owens holding his chest.

"Can you tell me what is the name of dis willage? . . . Dis willage? Does it have name? *Was heisst? Gutes Wasser? Warum?* Dis willage?"

Owens's eyes watering.

"Can you tell me what of these *kleine* trinkets are must for to have the having? Which one to you is a must-to-have, I mean to say . . ."

"Can you tell me where is the next Campings Platz? *Von hier?* In Dixie-Land National Forest? In Dixie-Land I'll park my van, no?"

It was good to get Owens out of the store.

At Red Gully what had been an exceedingly leisurely progress became a crawl. It took seven or eight breaks to get up it. I couldn't stand the claustrophobic, dismal place, and had to move on ahead. After too much waiting, I went back down to help drag the Cardiac Calf upward. Owens was not going to die on us today. No, not in Red Gully.

When Owens did croak it would be on the way to San Blas, Mexico, certainly, or on the beach there, circulating an umbrella drink, or maybe watching some stupid football game—he loved the Raiders—on his monumental TV, or maybe during the Jerry Lewis telethon. He'd start wondering why he didn't have a telethon of his own, then, winds blow, dust devils flog the poplars, tumbleweeds sail, and *pffft*.

The long train was coming fast, though not here, not today, please.

"*Wir wollen die Klipfen geklettern werden sein.*"

With Manny and Bird each holding an arm, Owens exited Red Gully. "If we could chust join Hans—"

"Hey, man, I'm okay. Just got to take some more aspirin and nitroglycerin. No problem. Wow, dig that view. Just a little 'a' and a bit o' nitro. Like a funny car . . . Like TNT . . ."

We tried to get him to sit down and take a breather.

But Owens wanted to go in search of Indian. And so he started going this way and that, with Bird and Manny following closely behind, or me, as per assignment—keeping an eye out. He wanted arrowheads and pottery shards and perhaps if he was lucky a big honking metate, *Hey, Bird, hey, Kevin, could you help me carry this down?* Maybe even an atlatl or pair of moccasins dry-docked for 800 years in a storage cyst. Lord knows there was plenty of Indian atop Joe's Mesa.

As we watched warily, we thought, let's get him down before he croaks: rolls over, seizes up, screams and tears at his shirt, at the gigantic motherfucking elephant on his chest, and then just this: full stop. No bloody ride to Provo. No air evacuation to Grand Junction.

Just a few minutes' slideshow of his final moments. Carla, his sad-eyed good wife, would be no help to him now. His son. The stepchildren. Daddy on the veranda of the Arm and Leg in sepia. Mama calling him to dinner. No, Owens would be gone to the Lower Sonoran to see the pinprick flowers of February, and then on to San Blas . . .

But it didn't turn out that way. After he stuffed his pockets full of lithic scatter, we nudged and prodded Owens down the gully, over the big bulges, around the ledge, through the talus, past the dead horse, down the last purple-green nuggety slippery slope, and onto the flat below.

It was getting late in the day. Bird was all for building a huge fire and spending the night. "Plenty of firewood on the flat, that's for sure. Nothing pressing back home. Might as well just hang, you guys. We've got all the water, booze, and food we need. Just feel this backpack.

But Manny said, "No, we won't have to do that. No, actually, we'll just carry on."

Owens wondering if there was any Indian on the flat. "There's no way they didn't camp here. There's no way there isn't something really good around here."

Me wondering how many hours it will take to get back to the car but glad to be adopted by the clan.

It took many hours, but nobody died. We avoided staying out like Bird always wanted to: warm front, back frozen, leaning against a rock or pile of wood, sitting in a bowl of cold sand, feeding twisty logs on the fragrant-burning, ever-popping, all-night-long white-man's fire, because you know life is so boring it takes a little risk to keep it spicy.

We embraced at the parking area. It was nearly dark.

We made it back, stardust and golden.

Two Chairs

November 1993. The windows are frozen shut. All night a cast-iron kettle boiled on the woodstove. The kettle is a low-tech humidifier that seals 'em up tight. The clearest, coldest mornings always follow a night of storm. Deer tracks slice through the new snow outside in the pasture. Snow crystals glimmer, prismatic. I have no desire to go outside yet, nor does the cat. We'll perch, watch, and wait for it to warm up a little.

Past an old log fence and through a screen of silver maples, I can see the Roylance home. Gloria passed away a year and a half ago, Ward last month. The Roylances were my neighbors and friends. Beyond the roof of their home they called Entrada rise the snow-frosted red cliffs they loved.

Their house smelled like wood smoke and wind. They were getting old, but not that old. It seems impossible to imagine Good Water without them.

In the 1970s, Ward and Gloria realized one of their dreams: to make their home in Wayne County, Utah. Wayne County is endowed with great and varied natural beauty, from the remnant Hudsonian forest growing to the top of 11,000-foot peaks to the twisted and every-hued canyons of the Dirty Devil. Ninety-six percent of Wayne County is public land, mainly Park Service, Forest Service, and BLM. Take Canyonlands or the Grand Canyon—there's scenery on the grand yet overdone scale, the Beethoven or Wagner scale, as Ward would say. Scenery around here is equally grand but surely more subtle, more richly colored, also of more manageable relief, not quite so exaggerated, but certainly well done and infinitely various. It hooks you.

The Roylances literally *made* their home here, designed and built Entrada with their own hands, and did so when they were in their fifties. Entrada sits on a cottonwood-covered lot, bordered on two sides by the Good Water canal, and it resembles a giant teepee, with five massive spruce logs supporting a steep-pitched, cedar-shake-covered roof. As in everything they did, they seemed to go out of their way to make its construction as difficult as possible.

Good Water would be nothing but sage and rabbit brush without irrigation. Because of its high elevation (6,850 feet) and short growing season, about the only things that thrive are pasture grass and alfalfa. From the east, after you drive up the long corroded hill from Fruita, past Egyptian cliffs and barren ledges, Good Water always provides a pleasant, pastoral relief. The town is an oasis, with tall trees overhanging Main Street and fields stretching to the barriers of rim rock and mountain. The town literally sits on the edge of the earth, or at least on the edge of the Colorado Plateau—it's all downhill from here.

A person can love the canyon country and want to sleep beneath cliffs, on ledges, in alcoves, on sand, but it's more soothing to awaken among trees.

The Roylances disliked labels. Nevertheless, they were perhaps the first environmentalists to inhabit, or reinhabit, Wayne County. They were generally despised by the local people, called names, threatened and ostracized, but they were admired by others who knew their writings and photographs of southern Utah's canyon country. Ward was best known for a guidebook, *Utah: A Guide to the State*. He was a Utah specialist and wrote many articles and books about his home state. In 1986 he self-published his spiritual autobiography, *The Enchanted Wilderness: A Red Rock Odyssey*. Gloria and Ward also produced two videos called *Art in Stone*.

The Roylances were urbane and civilized but unpretentious people, well read and well traveled. Ward had an impressive head of white hair. We sometimes kidded him that he ought to grow a beard so he would look more like an Old Testament prophet. There was quite a bit of the prophet in him, a voice crying in and for the wilderness. There was nothing of the profit in him; if he liked you, or if he thought you had the "right" environmental ideas, he'd give you the shirt off his back. He was too guileless for his own good.

Gloria was fussy about her appearance and often insisted on wearing makeup, a wig, and an attractive scarf before she would run errands up-county or even journey into her beloved red rock backcountry. Gloria was philosophically inclined, and her tendency toward seeing the bigger picture, as well as her broader direction—beyond mere partisanship—was essential to their collaboration.

One of Ward's favorite words was *ineffable*. No doubt he picked up a camera because words often fail to do justice to landscape and experience. So does film, though Ward had an excellent, truth-telling eye. Words and images alike frustrated him. If only the greatness of one's vision, the emotional power of one's experience, would equate to the greatness of pen and lens . . . but alas, Ward knew that he had never truly captured "the ineffable," that thing *out there* that can't be caught. He'd glimpsed it, seen its tracks, heard its voice, smelled it, but it had escaped. It always would and always will.

Ward had also seen others with more luck or more talent, less grand ideas, better connections or better schmoozing skills become better known and more successful. If Ward spent too much time just staring at the sky, melancholy and frustrated, Gloria kept him grounded.

They met and married when they were in their forties. Unquestionably, for both of them, the union was their life's fulfillment, a union that lasted twenty-five years.

You can learn interdependency, living on the edges.

Panguitch-born Wayne Owens was the only Utah politician of the last forty years to do anything for wilderness designation in the Beehive State. I recall a public meeting held in Loa, hosted by Representative Owens, who was defending his wilderness bill before a hostile audience. I was weary of having Wayne and his bill slandered, so I stood up and said, "Howdy, neighbors. I pay property tax to educate your children and I support wilderness." I then went on with some windy talk about preserving ecosystems and the importance of biodiversity. I might as well have told them that the future lay in child pornography, tofu, and communism.

When Ward stood up, someone shouted, "Shoot him!"

Unflustered, Ward delivered an eloquent speech, defending wilderness designation, telling his neighbors that if they didn't want wilderness *for themselves*, they should at least consider it *for the sake of their children.*

Take my word for it, the locals thought they were. Most seemed to believe that only by keeping the traditional economic ways and uses—mining, logging, and public-lands grazing—would there be any jobs for their children. Never mind that few of those present would be *directly* impacted by wilderness designation, if one of them would be, all of them would be.

Part of the debate was linguistic. While many urbanites see "wilderness" as an untrammeled place that is savagely holy, where for a few days a year they can rediscover, refine—indeed, redeem themselves—the general rural populace that depends on resource extraction sees "wilderness" as the most absurd and unproductive idea ever to come out of Washington, D.C. There is simply no middle ground. You're with us or you ain't.

Near the end of the meeting, Owens asked for a vote. Fully one-third of the people there (including a number of government agency people) raised their hands in support of 5.7 million acres of *additional* wild land in southern Utah.

A local woman, Cula Ekker, said, "Where did *they* come from?"

It must have seemed worse than a plague of locusts—a bunch of damned environmentals packing meetings in Loa. Rep. Owens went away sanguine from a meeting that *was* packed. While I was delighted to be among the few, I knew that a countywide referendum would have been something in the neighborhood of 97 percent against 3 percent. Not that numbers really mattered in the late 1980s, when Bill Clinton and his lock-up-o-rama were in nobody's wildest dreams.

Wilderness, land of no use. In our minds so be it.

There's no point in belaboring the conflict between insider and outsider, local and newcomer—the conflict is irresolvable. Yet it is a conflict that the Roylances, and anyone who spends any time living in southern Utah outside of Moab, has to deal with daily.

Ward put it well when he wrote, "Wayne County does not afford a rich social diet for those who are not church goers." It doesn't afford a rich social diet, period. You make your own entertainment or do without. It does keep the trendy rabble away.

I've come to agree with what Gloria would always say, "You know, they [the locals] see things differently than you or I do."

Where some see a beautiful and twisted pinyon, others see good firewood. And whenever I'm reminded of Winged Victory of Samothrace when staring at a venerable juniper, I recall that one of my neighbors likes to say he's been fighting them damned cedars his whole life.

The Roylances were not the gung-ho, wilderness-as-playground, hey-dude, high-adventure types. Ward was plagued by bad hips, and Gloria was never much of a hiker. They liked nothing more than to drive *slowly* through wild lands, stop frequently, exult, and take photographs. They practiced gentle use, use that doesn't diminish the land or the visitor.

There can be more secrets in 200 yards than ten miles. It's all in how you look.

When the artistic impulse combines with affection, remarkable things can result. It's for their collaboration that I want Ward and Gloria to be remembered. Two stood stronger than one.

Ward was prone to melancholy. Like most dreamers, he tended to take the many slights and reverses that life deals personally. He was often discouraged by the recalcitrance of the locals, the battles fought and lost, as well as his own lack of recognition— or the lack of recognition of his ideals. Ward was no egoist and eschewed literary limelight to a fault, but he fervently believed that the Colorado Plateau—as a region—was unique, whole, holy, and worthy of the highest protection.

I remember the way Ward would run his hands through his hair when he was upset, or rub them together. Gloria would look at him as a mother studies an errant son, glance down for a moment, smile as if to regain *their* composure, and then work on changing the subject.

Gloria buoyed people up. "Well," she would say, "I can't help it; I'm an optimist. In time things will change. We know so many good people who care."

But she was not a blind optimist and, unlike a dreamer such as Ward, Gloria was a better judge of people. More level headed and certainly more world savvy, Gloria gave Ward both the courage and direction he needed.

Gloria filled a spiritual gap as well. Ward had lost the Mormon faith of his upbringing, and Gloria had showed him the way to a type of romantic pantheism, a high-desert Druidism, a belief that all things had souls and were beings. Gloria had a catholic interest in religion and sought knowledge of Eastern religion and ritual as well as Native American spirituality to broaden her understanding of the world. Allied with this was her *wild* aesthetic sensibility: that "natural" objects—rocks, roots, landscape—were worthy of the same type of contemplation and possessed the same vocabularies of response as man-made *objets d'art*. Gloria found her god, not the devil, in the details. From the first notion came the Roylance's idea of *The Enchanted Wilderness*. The second idea they explored in their videos.

The aesthetic of nature-as-art propelled and informed their activist thinking. One can support the idea of wilderness for several reasons: it is good to preserve places for ecological or scientific reasons, it is a redemptive playground, it is a church and sacred, it can keep us sane and remind us how things used to be, but Ward and Gloria saw especially the art in it. You don't build a natural gas well in the middle of MOMA, do you? Then why are people so bent on destroying the vision? Profit, dimness, heritage, laziness—there are many reasons. But to the Roylances it was a great artistic exhibition out there, a place to feel and love and leave alone in perpetuity.

The Roylances were the type of people that stick with you, partly because they were so *different*.

One splendid early autumn day, they took Dora and me out to view one of their favorite places, Factory Bench: a barren, lunar place that is bleak as can be from a distance but holds many secrets up close.

We parked our trucks (they called their Ford Yellow Bird) and made our way to "the Gallery," an acre or two of golden-ocher stones on rock pedestals. The diversity of shapes was astounding.

"I know these fellows," Gloria said as she walked around and touched her "rock art." She had taken people to see her totems countless times.

Ward grew emotional as he looked around at the huge sweep of landscape—from the Henry Mountains to the San Rafael—Roylance Land. "Don't you just love this country?"

It was no rhetorical question but an interrogatory of bone and blood.

As we walked back to the road, I found a shot-up roadsign facedown in a wash. I turned it over. It read "Range Cattle." Gloria, Dora and I laughed at the irony. *Please don't shoot them free-roaming beeves!* But Ward was disgusted. "Those people don't even know what they're doing."

The shot-up range cattle sign now hangs on a wall in my basement. Statement art and found art can lead us into troublesome country, but this sign is a true beauty. I would not, however, hang it in Wayne County. Not these days.

Often when we were down in the dumps about bleak economic prospects—enough money to start a house, not enough to finish it—and the fact that there were already plenty of carpenters and maids in Wayne County, not to mention writers and painters, we'd go over to the Roylances for a pep talk. We circled the wagons, just as the more indigenous people did. We'd rant about the current outrage: the latest timber sale (in those days, serious consideration was being given to cutting 70 percent of the trees on the mammoth flat top of Boulder Mountain), or the less-than-sporting hunting method of baiting bears with offal and donuts, or chasing and treeing cougars with hounds. Gloria always brought us back to earth by reminding us how alike we were—trying to build a house by ourselves, loving the country, wanting to live in a beautiful place. There was strength in that house, even in small numbers.

The two extant Roylance videos, *Art in Stone,* are slow paced and filled with stunning visual images, twenty-five years of images. They lead one to contemplation. Yet the trend in current canyon-country video is toward displaying fast-paced gravity sports, aerial shots of buttes and bottoms, and time-lapse footage of clouds: in other words, earth-based *fromage.* The Roylance videos never sold well, and when the marketing arm of the National Park Service pulled them from their shelves, Ward took it personally.

Gloria, as always, was more philosophical. "We put everything we could into those videos," she'd say. "We did what we had to do, and we're satisfied with the results."

Timing: horses at dusk, tenebrous shadows flying across the flat on last night's snow, seem out of time these days, too.

Gloria had worked for years in retail sales and had many "people" skills that her husband lacked. Gloria's was an older, wiser soul than Ward's, I think, and Ward in many ways remained a kind of adolescent. Still, his passion and her restraint created a kind of magical synchronicity.

Because Ward was prone to melancholy and diffidence, he couldn't schmooze to save his life. What little public recognition he received came very late. Recently, a market has opened in literary dude-ing, hosting workshops and conferences in scenic places, trying to attract dilettantes with money by being facile and positive.

The Roylances might have headed that way; it's hard to say. They were never very mercenary. It would have been difficult for them to call a turd a honeybee.

Still, Ward and Gloria never lost their proselytizing zeal. In the early 1970s, they formed and financed the Enchanted Wilderness Association, a group dedicated to the idea that the Colorado Plateau should be seen as an ecological whole, worthy of study and protection. For a variety of reasons, the idea didn't catch on.

In the late 1980s, partly as a result of trying to get citizen support to stop the proposed dam on the Fremont River, Ward, Gloria, Dora, and I tried to establish the Fremont River Arts Council, admittedly a front group. That idea also foundered. "Arts Council" was assuredly a suspicious term that translated in the Wayne County vernacular as "stuck-up fairies." What is art and who is doing the council-ing? It may have been as bad as "wilderness," a land of no use, or for that matter Earth Day, which has become "Wise-Use Day" in the public schools of Wayne County. You've got to know your audience, and we didn't.

I would suggest that the Roylances belonged to other times. Their sensibility was truly Romantic. Others might feel the sort of ecstasy they expressed in nature, but many forces corrode the modern Romanticism. Sometimes today to gush is also to blush. You must remember that this was the late '80s, early '90s, the time of the Gulf War I. We were a long way from the man from Hope, Arkansas, and Bruce Babbitt. The sad fact is that the Roylances were just on the edge of being understood and accepted—not so much for their ideas, for aestheticians are not generally well appreciated, but for their prescience—to lock the land up in bunches—when they died. Perhaps they belonged to no particular time at all, but to the eternal past, present, and future, the "real time" of high desert land.

They would certainly have rejoiced in Bill Clinton's magnum opus: Grand Staircase-Escalante National Monument, something they dreamed of but could never have pulled off.

After Gloria passed, Ward was inconsolable. He felt the closeness of his spouse, and said he talked to her often from the other side. She was still present in every detail of the house—the handmade fireplace rock displays, the roots-as-art pieces, the woodworking dioramas around the windows, the stained glass.

If you gamble on a homemade house in the country and follow your own drummer, the business world doesn't really care a rat's ass about how well composed these things are—it's just something to bulldoze and start again, and it leaves you with nothing when your wife isn't there.

Whenever I visited with him, the gloom was thick. I had my own divorce to contend with, so we were two pretty glum hombres, and honestly, I was having a hard time just getting my own air; Ward Roylance was not the healthiest of company. He said he was tired, tired of fighting and losing, tired of battling against implacable, ignorant foes. He said he wanted to leave environmental battles to the younger people. He also sensed his own time wasn't long.

In the meantime, the vultures had begun to circle. The Roylances had no children or direct heirs. A group of people from Salt Lake began to cultivate Ward, seeming to be in search of a guru. Ward was undoubtedly lonely, and these new friends provided companionship and recognition. I repeatedly warned him that their motives might not be purely good, that they might be after his property.

Ward set up a type of foundation, without an endowment, that would be run by himself, one relative, and the Salt Lakers. Once he was gone, however, his newfound friends, holding an easy majority, would be able to do whatever they pleased.

It's still chilly at noon. I stroll over to the Roylance place to pay my respects and say good-bye. The wind, as it often does, is howling out of the west, so lingering is doubly painful. I walk the Entrada grounds, huddle in the lee of trees and buildings, and sense I will not be welcome here as before. Nevertheless, the spirit of the occupants still remains, in the trees they tended, in the view of the Cockscomb, in their collections of rocks, and in the house that was truly a home.

Fresh snow shines on the southern slopes of Thousand Lake Mountain, their favorite, most spiritually charged place, and I feel sharply the separation, the absence of two remarkable people, a team of two visionaries, two friends.

On the September–trimmed lawn beside their house, two empty old-fashioned lawn chairs, turned inward, face north.

Wild Currants

THREE LOMBARDY POPLARS BRUSH TIPS, sway in the pre-dawn breeze. Beyond the poplars stand lines of barren cottonwoods, pasture hedges, eighty feet tall. The sky lightens. The tangled upper limbs of the cottonwoods form a lattice against the sweep of vibrant pastels. Soon the entire sky is robin-egg blue, crepuscular blue, Dora's blue.

I don't think Dora is in Wayne County now. I don't know where she is and I pretend I don't care. I have returned to the scenes of our crimes. I have been sleeping in the garden.

Today is December 21. A worn year dying, a new one being born. What's to celebrate? There ought to be something. I believe I'll sip coffee and tease the cat, look outside and concentrate on something beside the bad country song going round and round in my head. Eight hours of daylight stretch before me. I will do no chores today, fix no fences. I will sift, scan the cloudless sky, remember. The pull of a place such as this is strong.

—

Every such story has two sides. You didn't ask, but I said it was all my fault. No, I didn't. Okay, then, it's all my fault. Two sides: do dirt and get done dirt. Wait a minute. What did I do to deserve this? And what about the other side? It is certainly not all my fault. It's hers. Go ahead and ask her.

No, don't. This is my story, and I'll tell it like it is. Like it was.

—

Only a fool would plant fruit trees at such an altitude. Nearly all Good Waterites are fools of long standing. Every homestead has a pocket orchard. Every couple of years most fruit trees escape the May frosts and bear a prodigal crop. The noble tradition of fruit trees in Good Water is an expression of hope, a denial of realities, that old western thing again. Or maybe it's a tradition for the birds.

The garden, a fenced rectangle of red and vermilion dirt, measures fifteen paces by fifty-five. The soil varies from deep shaley clay to the rich leavings of an old sheep corral. Red dirt presents an irony to the gardener: red soil means the soil is rich in iron, but bushes and trees cannot process it. Ammonium sulfate or chelated iron must be added to the soil.

Four years ago I planted a dwarf Elberta peach tree, and I swear it actually shrank. Aggressive addition of these minerals caused the tree to finally shoot up last summer and bear one mammoth peach. It then promptly died. It just up and died.

—

My true friends tell me someday it won't sting—that I'll see the problems weren't mainly with me. I'll stop feeling sorry for myself and acting like I'm the only one this has ever happened to.

—

A gardener works, a gardener hopes. A gardener eliminates high steppe grasses so that his own weeds may grow instead. Plant beneath May's darkened moon, water at dusk and dawn, wait. Surprises thrive: wind and rain, ditch water and birds bring seeds of ragweed and dandelion, burdock, and thistle, but also wild currants, squawbush, wild rose.

—

I have been living in Richmond, Utah, seven miles from the Idaho border, attending graduate school at Utah State University, in well-watered Cache Valley, and coming to Good Water on holidays. I'm determined to make it the right choice. My new place has always had an old-clothes feel. My mother grew up in nearby Smithfield; our people are buried there. I have an adorable aunt and uncle who visit me.

I have been having three-way conversations lately in my many walks around Richmond. We take a lot of walks this way.

It's important, I think, not to be living here, in Good Water. There are too many memories, memories of her, of us. It's too close to the bone. I think I have options. I am determined to go someplace. I am determined to *make* myself into a good writer. Maybe too determined: writing can't be the most important thing in any valuable life. Or can it? I'm trying too hard, but I fancy it's all I've got.

Dora made a few attempts to come to Richmond. She cried a lot. She wouldn't let me touch her, my wife. What a fool I was! I ought to have known. Duh. Double duh. Maybe I didn't want to know. Denial works wonders, doesn't it?

If I could only see it today as a favor. Freedom. Even the time she—they—came to fetch her stuff. A Taiwanese twelve-speed, pots and pans, goblets and dishes, books, skis, a picture of the queen . . .

She said she wanted me to be there, maybe to rub my face in it. No, thanks! I left and climbed Mt. Tokewanna with a buddy. It proved to be a very long slog. We came down in the rain. The rain continued all the way across Wyoming and into northern Utah. There was all this noise in my head. Her stuff was gone. She left the ring.

—

The first year Dora and I were too busy building a house to garden. July days are long. You work until you can't think straight and then work some more.

We shopped at the Arm and Leg General Store just across the street or at the Bicknell Vegetable Morgue. We did without. We learned the first lessons of survival in Wayne, County—substitute or do without. You can't get fresh vegetables in Bicknell, but you can get liquor. For many, liquor assuages much. What liquor won't fix, baling wire and duct tape will. When these fail, there's always suspicion and hatred, which won't fix anything but which occupy the time until pies fall from the sky and light, clean industry comes magically to town, providing well-paying jobs for everyone's kids and preserving the traditional ways of life.

—

Mix love and nature and landmarks get marked, scented with the admixture. Dora and I ascended every prominent peak or spire I can see. We saw the frozen breath of elk rising in September, scrambled up buttes and made love on top. I will have to win the landmarks back, reclaim them for myself, for the future.

—

Folks here have an interesting habit of mind. Things they don't like don't exist. Change has swept over town like an August gully washer sweeps down from the slopes of Thousand Lake Mountain. Poverty Flat is becoming rich in newcomers, and we newcomers have strange ways.

Newcomers display junk as trophies: wagon wheels and Fresno scrapers, singletree harnesses and cow skulls. My eastern neighbors host an exhibition of useless farm implements in their yard: mowers and hay rakes, hand plows, a leaning scythe or two, a milking stanchion, a cement mixer, and even an old kid's saddle they bring out and flop down on the hitching post for special occasions.

Few still ranch or farm on the flat. The land has become too valuable. Ranchers sell out to the town's one realtor, who has a knack of finding the right reinhabitants. The old ways are gone forever. The useful become ornamental. This is called the New West.

The most prominent relict in the garden is Walt Smith's old hayrack, a platform of sun-bleached ponderosa planks bolted to a frame of fir logs. For years this hayrack was dragged around Smith's fields, stacked to the groaning point with feed. These days it provides a fine platform from which to view the gaudy sunsets. Two wild currant bushes have grown up between the planks.

In front of the compost bin reposes the front wheel of a #7 McCormick-Deering tractor, rusted local color, at least fifty years old. I'm fond of the wheel and what it represents: Fortune, the seasons, birth and decay—you know, it's a symbol. Anyone with any sense sees just junk.

—

The second year proved good for gardening. Fresh salads often graced our table. We enjoyed a few ears of just-off-the-stalk corn, too, but the night before we were going to harvest and freeze our half bushel, several deer jumped the fence, helped themselves to the corn, and pruned the fruit trees. It made me pretty sore.

I've never had great fondness for deer; they are too common and usually too skittish. The Good Water bambi are brazen as well. They waltz into folks' front yards as if they have a right. I fervently prayed some hunter would do for those corn-fed bambi when the season was right. Since then, I've never planted corn. All my deciduous trees are protected by sheep fence. The gardener learns.

I'd rather see horses in my pasture. Horses beautify the landscape generally and provide a reason to irrigate, but the greatest pleasure of irrigation is that it attracts half the birds in the county, grackles and cowbirds, robins and blackbirds, killdeers and bobwhites. It's a type of dues payment, unearthing so many worms.

On irrigation day the cat, Lamont, would sit morosely at the window not wanting to wet his paws. So many birds, such short summers. The dog, Joe Notom, would go blithely loco, racing up and down the furrows, leaping across ditches, biting foam and bubble, scaring the birds, and generally getting so much mud on his wirehair coat that all that distinguished him from sodden terra firma were two yellow-orange ovals of delighted dog eyes. I got the cat, Dora the dog.

—

We got married high up in Big Cottonwood Canyon on a lovely June day in the old Civilian Conservation Corps shelter at the Spruces. This proved unwise. For fifteen years Big Cottonwood Canyon was absolutely my favorite place in the world, for hiking, skiing, fishing, whatever. I can't go back there now.

—

We moved directly from Hoboken to Good Water. People say it must have been quite a change. Yes and no. Good Water, like Hoboken, is an edge community. Both places offer high points from which to gaze upon a sublime spectacle: the towers and canyons of Manhattan, corporate and cultural Yosemite, or the domes, spires, and escarpments of the Waterpocket Fold. The sensations of wonder, of awe, are not that different.

Everything is allowed. Good Water is a great town for outlaws and drunks, always has been. I was drunk, so were all my friends; it's easier that way. The outlaw spirit is still palpable just beyond the town limits.

To find and frequent the periphery is imperative for the artist, and dangerous—the margin is a sucking whirlpool. A short step adds an emotional margin to a geographical one. It's all downhill from here.

—

Summer: the misty blue chords of Gershwin's "Summertime" and open-air dinners. Beneath a sky filled with sheets of shining virga, Dora and I would feast on thin-sliced London broils grilled over a ponderosa and juniper fire, dirt-fresh salads of lettuce, beets, carrots, peas, and new potatoes boiled in their tender red skins. Vegetables of our labors. Good times, satiated times, lucky times.

The pull of a place such as this is strong. One dawn, one still afternoon, one walk in the pygmy forest brings back the tug. But living here full-time was a constant struggle for lucre. Maybe it's better, cleaner, to work somewhere else and come here to revive, purify, and play.

—

Wild currants thrive along Walt Smith's old fences. The berries taste like finest sherry. Old-timers say wild currants make excellent preserves, but one has to be quick—the birds know when the berries are ripe, too.

All birds are welcome here, but that does not mean they are safe. Killdeer nest in the pasture. Robins have nested in the old outhouse. A pair of dusky flycatchers raised two broods under the eaves of this building last summer. I feel obligated to feed the birds, and do, my justification for working on the farm. It's the least I can do, as Lamont nullifies too many of my good intentions, sometimes bringing in a squawking flicker, a thrush, or a fetching American goldfinch during dinner. I do feel guilty, but accomplice guilt is different from being caught red-handed. Or is it? Guilt's a noxious weed, anyway, highly invasive.

—

We planted a large garden the fourth year, but there was something in the soil, some blight, some spreading white fungus, that attacked the rows of tomatoes and potatoes and stole the crop.

Still, the salad vegetables did well, especially the peas and lettuce. I was working out of town most of the summer and left Dora to tend the garden. I returned home on weekends, but something didn't seem quite right. At summer's end, I went to Wyoming to revisit the Wind River Mountains after too many years away. Dora didn't want to come; she had begun cultivating a different garden plot in a nearby town.

We had planned to leave Good Water that fall for graduate school in Logan. Autumn came in early, the aspen flamed on the slopes of Boulder Mountain. I left, alone. Dora stayed.

—

It could, of course, have been anyone. I tried not to say, "I would never," and so on. Life is a wheel. Still, since it wasn't the mailman, but rather my best friend, I guess the betrayal seemed double.

—

The last trip together was up to Paradise Flat with Jim and Sandy. Because it's such a rocky road up there, no one goes up to Paradise often, and the views are truly remarkable, big-time, grand: the whole overcolored desert land is laid out at your feet, a reality map of all that might matter, not a settlement of any kind *out there*, just rock and more rock, stretching to Rio Colorado, then beyond the river, pink and mauve, blue and gray, buff and rust and dun, castles and temples and canyons tilted and twisted, wilder than goshawks as seen from 9,000 feet on the rockiest road around.

Dora was pouring down beers like there was no tomorrow. I drove and tried to ignore the obvious. I felt certain that by not drinking I could change things, could change myself, the outcome. But what I couldn't change was the dead body in the back of the truck, the dead deer that lined the road, the vultures circling that we could not leave behind. Nevertheless, we put on our game faces and danced around our history. We set up camp in the rocks and buck brush. Dora puked out the tent door.

—

Driving out was worse. If we were granted two days' reprieve from limbo, we knew we had to go back down, to return to the mess we'd made. Dora was driving, wasn't paying real close attention, drifted into a sandy trench, and we got good and stuck—to the back hubs, even though we were going downhill. Getting stuck is common in this country. There's no point in blame. It could happen to anyone.

After a quarter hour of digging, Good Water innkeeper Southey Swede, out for a little drive, happened along. He pulled us out. We drove back to town in silence, both avoiding the stark symbolism.

—

Unable to sleep, I walked outside and stared at the moon. Finally it was clear enough to me—there was no choice in what I had to decide and do. Enough limbo had passed, and I knew it was time to try to let it go and move on to the next stage, whatever that might be.

Maybe she was relieved. Maybe it was as painful as she said it was. Maybe I should stop caring what she thought. Maybe that was the problem. Maybe there's nothing more to say about it.

We said good-bye to maybes in the morning.

—

The sun reaches its apex low on the southern horizon. I step outside to take the air and smell burning cedar, the piquant odor of wintertime. The garden has an old sweater feel. My feet have worn a path through it to the outbuilding, 100 paces of a lazy, curving S. I can walk it in the dark by touch.

The path attests to my presence, so do the buildings and trees, but was it I who did these things? Another I. I have buried that person. Like hell I have. That I, the out-of-it I, the bloodshot I, lies in the compost bin alongside the other Is of my life. Gone, not so easily forgotten.

—

I've got to do something, so taking a shovel, hoe, and rake, I clear pasture grass and alfalfa from the south side of the studio—I'll plant flower seeds next spring. As I finish spading, I hear the distant honking of geese, unmistakable as Elvis. Two vees of them wheel over town. I count forty-four. Unsteady vees against the afternoon sky—they merge and part in crazy patterns. They pass to the east, turn, pass overhead again, run, pass over, turn, and eventually disappear in the west. I see it as auspicious.

—

Sunset, same colors as dawn. To the east, in the absolute top of a Lombardy poplar, a solitary great horned owl is calling. The air is still, the song carries. A crepuscular bird, the great horned owl, *Bubo virginianus*. Twilight washes in, a deep blue vault above the almost-black wall of Boulder Mountain. I can see my breath now. It's time to go inside and start a fire.

Bonita Bacchanalia

LIVING IN WAYNE COUNTY IS LIKE LIVING IN WYOMING IN this regard: everyone is at least mildly bipolar, especially in winter. Weather and isolation are largely to blame. Day follows day of incessant gusty wind, accompanied by feckless high-hatted rattling, with never enough of the white stuff to show for it. Then arrive a couple of snow-kissed cold calm days, cloudy banked with the threat that it will soon start up again, like gunshots on opening day. And it does: the awful pounding of the all-night wind, the sickening sucking sound of the edge over yonder, the whirlpool wrack of lost souls, the distant muffled drowning cries, the smoke down the chimney. These factors contribute to a feeling of general despair.

Get through a winter with only a woodstove and nothing seems impossible anymore.

Antsy-ness and cabin fever set in. Some days you find yourself down in the sand-swept flats of Hanksville, digging out after a three-day blow. And then sometimes you're up on Donkey Point looking down, or if not on the very edge of Donkey Point, you're following a skid path toward it, with a hurt ankle, an empty stomach, fighting off gnats, deer flies, and mosquitoes. And sometimes you're just a donkey, so when, at last, sighing "Uncle" from the woodpile, the thought of a trip to Richfield, its meager blandishments, fills the mind and heart with joy, then you know Wayne County has worked its magic on you.

And so it is that the people gather together in celebration, to shunt the ghosts, find a cohort in the suffering, and break it down and carry on.

There is a party. Everyone is there. At Manny's. There's a band playing in the living room, the Good Water Band, and the band is playing mainly cover tunes with long spacey jams thrown in. The drummer is handsome and sings some vocals. He is so handsome that one of his fans, an insane married woman, thinks he might be the reincarnation of Orpheus or Apollo. She wrote him many postcards elucidating her theory, postcards that were passed around and posted on the bulletin board of the P.O. The bass player smokes too many cigarettes and has a dark side. He has worked at every restaurant in the county, but only for a season.

The guitar player is a rednecked hippie who sometimes channels Jerry G., and he sings vocals too, as does his wife, a nightmare hippie girl who wields a tambourine with menace and flips her hair in enravishing ways.

Since this is a small town, guests sit in and jam: San Re with the lengthy record who plays blues harp with such fervor and conviction that it gives goose bumps and simultaneously alerts his probation officer living in a farmhouse in Monroe, and Zeke, one of the Good Water kids, who will do homage to Jimi and Stevie Ray, and that's Alice is in the corner smacking spoons, and Carole is shout-singing along, drink sloshing, and if the band only had a keyboardist to fill up the space in between or perhaps a saxophone to underscore the melee, this would be the greatest house band in America today, and its loud, and in the living room, part of the living room, and people are shouting, everyone is shouting.

Everyone is shouting and smoking cigarettes and drinking, and there's maybe 100 people in Manny's house, and it is not a particularly large house, but it's a real kick-ass party, turned up to 11, and also very loud. A house full of prospective DUIs. A county attorney's dream team. Where's Manny?

Manny is listening to Owens's rant in the kitchen. Something about the municipal water system. It's always about water. The municipal water system is Owens's clogged left ventricle. In the kitchen everyone is shouting. The town's mayor is in the kitchen, shouting, also his wife, a former mayor. Why are they shouting? They are shouting so people will listen to them. There's a band playing in the living room. Everyone has opinions and opinions are good to share.

Many believe Manny is the best carpenter in town. His kitchen is a marvel of Manny style: thick-cut slabs of ponderosa pine, rustically elegant—yellow pine everywhere: handmade cabinets, whorlly countertops, mitered planks—all finished with many coats of polyurethane, a good varnish to apply while drinking.

Manny's greatness has never been seriously questioned, except by Bird, who seems preternaturally inclined to question Manny's greatness, which complicates matters since Anna is Manny's sister and Bird's lady. Bird and Manny are fighting again, so Bird is not in the kitchen shouting, he is in the living room shouting. People are shouting around Manny. I need to go outside for some fresh air.

But Anna catches me up. She's different from her brother. Manny is reserved and maybe a bit chilly. Anna is effusive. She pulls me into a dark room and locks the door behind us. It's the second bedroom, now a storage room. It was Marielle's room but

Marielle died, and that was bad for Manny and Anna Lee and Marielle. She talks about her but doesn't cry. She checks the door. It was all pretty messed up, she says.

I can't remember how many late nights I've called on Anna and Bird, and they never seemed to mind, just move it forward. Okay, maybe I have been a user and lonely, but we really did meld together in good and silly ways. I've seldom been alone with her. It wasn't that Bird was controlling or psycho about it, it just turned out that way, and Manny and Bird were my elders in the hippie clan, with Owens, and Anna was my sister, and I'm alone with her, and there's a party with about 100 shouting people just outside the door. Anna is tall with brown-green eyes and blond hair. I would like to kiss her because I love her. I tell her I love her. I love you, Anna Lee, I say. Whatever, she says. But I love her like a sister, but I can't say I love you like a sister, Anna Lee, because I never had a sister like you. It's easy to love her. She says wait a minute, Chester. It's not like that, I say. I just love you. That's cool, she says. I love you too, I guess. Shall we enjoy another?

The band starts playing again. I decide to make the round and rounds. I can see several of the Good Water Bitches in one tableau. They call themselves the Good Water Bitches, I don't and wouldn't. I call them the Good Water Lady Friends when I get to be part of their coven. I want to say right now that I know the GWBs intimately, so to say, as their token male. Out at Alice's. Over at Carole's. With Connie. A token male, and because I'm damaged goods and divorced from someone they sort of know, it's safe and cool. One time I brought Alice some flowers from the garden, and that was considered sensitive by the GWBs, whose men bring them elk and deer if they're lucky. Actually I have a new love but she is far away, and I can be with the GWBs in a harmless platonic way, because in point of fact much of my heritage is tied up in roping in several women, plural wives, a sisterhood over which

I am entitled to preside, so I'm not uncomfortable with that role. And maybe they want to figure out what went wrong with Dora and me, and maybe they know. When they have covens there's supper and games and snacks and liquor, and at some point I will go home and they will stay, moving on to stronger things.

I haven't had a drink in eighteen months, yet at this time I cannot claim sobriety. In the other bedroom, there's this guy from Boulder who is talking about a car wreck, his fourth bad one. He likes to drive bitchin' Camaros and get in car wrecks. And he's talking about how in the last one the skin on his scalp got cut right across his eyebrows and pulled back, like the skin on an orange, just sliced like this right here—he shows us—but his skull was fine, it turned out, and when his buddies found him, red-splattered and bleeding out, they just kind of slapped the big flap down, wiped it off with a spare T-shirt, and sealed it up with some duct tape—you have to go along the seam and press it together—he demonstrates—a one-shot thing, what with how sticky that damned duct tape is—and they just happened to have some duct tape in the car, duh, and because his blood was all coagulated ("cogulated") mostly they made out fine, thank goodness for that, and the rescuers earned praise from the ER doctor in Panguitch, and now he wears a headband, figures maybe there's a business opportunity in it, so he's going to market his own special brand of stylish and specially absorbent headbands, and that's enough for me.

I run into Geno Hops who once helped me with the simplest possible phrase—"There's nothing wrong with *you*"—so deliciously weighted in meaning, at a time when I needed to hear something simple like that, and I say, hey Geno, it's good to see you, bro, and Carole is sing-shouting along with the band, drink sloshing, and Manny is in the hallway, *What a party, man*, and that's Bird in the corner: I love your girlfriend slash common-law wife, Bird, like a sister, and San Re the nearly blind hippie is playing again, and when he plays the room goes fairly quiet because San Re channels all the oppressed, the downtrodden, and every blind blues harp player from Chicago to New Orleans, and that ends up being very strong medicine, 'cause he can go places in the cosmos few of us dare to tread, including, especially, his probation officer, and it's time for me to make my exit.

I walk very slowly down the lane to my place. When I turn around I notice that Manny's house is spinning round and round. I linger to watch it spin round and round.

Everyone inside there is shouting and doing some wild dervish dance with the spinning, holding on with the dogged determination of the damned. It's good I left when I did, and between the splatter of stars, the inky night, the crunch of gravel, and the necessity to take it all in, not to mention the Milky Way, it takes me half an hour to walk home, even if it's only a few hundred yards.

Crossing over the rock bridge and easing down the driveway, I softly think this is the place where I will die.

Here I go.

High Plateau Blues

i.

WAY, WAY UP THERE, JUST BELOW THE RIM CRAGS, is where trees grow thickest, making their own shade to nurture more trees. Up there rhyolite and andesite talus mingle with stands of too-tight timber, making a walk-through slow, snaky, miserable, and sour. Up there is where you learn to call it the Ugly, the Boulder Mountain Ugly, and you learn to avoid it: the long and the short of it, the always a part of it, the low-down high-country trouble of it, the dues you pay to get through it.

Having said all that, I do believe it's calling out to me.

You learn to know better, but it's pretty. And high. And alluring in its repellency. And hard to believe: the land of all these blues—conifers in dark shadows, lighter misty ridges, gayer bluebird skies—the ever-blue drapery of the southernmost holdings of Hudsonian forest, a cool zone in an otherwise cooked country.

Blues too because these slopes stand to remind: life and love tangled up in landscape, easy to get lost in. The blues: twelve bars and turnaround licks, with novelty in repetition, newness in the same old blue suede shoes.

Late in the day when the light is just right, those distant blue slopes seem near enough to touch.

Hand me down my walking cane.

—

These shades of blue are found most vividly in the high plateaus of south-central Utah. Tones that nod toward indigo but are never precisely flat black, not even at night when snipes, yes snipes, American snipes, serenade the dark hours in the neighbor's pasture, dropping down the scale in quarter notes.

During the monsoon lightning walks across the mountaintop, splitting the night sky into shards of misted blue ether.

In the early morning after the rains the high-washed slopes shine in aqua, then give way to a million trees in an efflorescence of blue—western-bluebird blue, bluebell blue, lupine blue, larkspur blue, caldera lake blue.

Reduced to lines on paper: four raven miles stretch from my back door to Boulder Cove, then rise one, two, three, four rough-and-tumble hours through the pygmy forest and onto gentler rising slopes of ponderosa, manzanita, and aspen. Then comes the Ugly and all its attendant troubles, followed by the rim crags— gateway to the mesa top, the mountaintop. Only a June day would be long enough for the whole of it.

Unlike most mountains, where trees thin with elevation gained, these spruce and fir tighten with height into groves of woe and bad times coming. The big blue mountain stands. Maybe it invites. Maybe not. Maybe it's enough to watch its many moods.

—

Looks are deceiving.

Geologists explain that Boulder Mountain and Thousand Lake Mountain were once one, that their former embrace was riven by cycles of glaciers building, then melting. Glaciers working their mojo in ice and gravity and carborundum and aggregate, melting into rivers that carried chunks and particles away.

From the top of Thousand Lake, just fifty feet higher than Boulder, a couple of miles further north, you can see how the theory might make sense—right at your feet. Let's accept the postulate. It also makes certain poetic sense.

But it cannot account for these green, green blues.

—

To put it down in spades: I first fell for this country because of the canyons, the red-range colors, the unexpected twist, but was drawn uphill for the cool in summer. From Poverty Flat the exuberance of red cliffs forms the middle ground with darker hills above. This clinches it: the eye is always drawn up.

—

Seen from space, or from the satellite images taken from space, the Fishlake, Awapa, Aquarius, Boulder, and Thousand Lake Plateauplex appears as a gigantic manta ray, with Poverty Flat, where all winds meet, at its mouth. The semicircle is the last southern stand of the high plateaus.

Names can be deceiving, too. Boulder and Thousand Lake are often called "flat-topped mountains," which sounds odd as mountains don't generally possess flat tops—not flat tops encompassing many square miles. They're not mesas either, because mesas are generally smaller and lack the mountainous raiment. Boulder Mountain is, in fact, recognized as North America's second-largest "flat-topped mountain," after Colorado's Grand Mesa, a designation that just serves to muddy the waters.

Some fools have called Boulder the "throne" of the Colorado Plateau, but it's a backless throne if it is one, not much of one if that, and it isn't. It's a table, a mesa, a bidet, a flattop, a mountain. If you can't in good conscience call these plateaus mountains, you must denote them mountainous and montane. Take off your blindfolds, look down and not around, and you're in the Sierra Nevada, the Wind Rivers, the Colorado Rockies, Yellowstone, Glacier.

—

Wrong names can be deceiving.

Take it a step further, though, and lose it all in the midday haze. The names of Boulder and Thousand Lake should be reversed. Apparently an early cartographer's gaffe is the cause, but like other gaffes it has remained—in print now and forever.

Proof? Boulder Mountain contains several dozen lakes on the glacial shelves below the rim, and many more on top. If we count potholes and ponds, yes, there are perhaps a thousand lakes on Boulder Mountain. Thousand Lake Mountain, on the other hand, sports only three decent-sized lakes, and perhaps a dozen smaller ones, although it does feature many billions of boulders. So do most mountains—flat topped or otherwise. Boulder should be Thousand Lake; Thousand Lake should be Boulder. They were once and ought to be again. What's in a name? Nothing more than identity.

—

To know the Ugly in daylight is one thing, to learn it at night another. For a time I worked as an independent contractor surveying the National Forest land for Mexican spotted owls. Like its cousin in the Pacific Northwest, the northern spotted owl, the mariachi variety of spotted owl was considered to be an indicator species, a critter that showed by its presence whether or not a forest or ecosystem was healthy. It was thought that the Mexican spotted owl favored old-growth forests, and if so, it might be useful as a tool to curtail logging. In actual fact, very little was known about the Mexican spotted owl, hence the need for these surveys.

On the job we followed a set protocol and surveyed each area at least four times. Routes were marked on topo maps, then checked in daytime for practicality, and then marked when needed—in the case of cross-country, hard-to-follow routes—with bright nylon road survey flags to keep hooters (some of us preferred to be called "surveyors") from getting lost.

An hour before sunset a crew of hooters would drive to an appointed spot, split up, walk the routes, and meet back up hours later at an agreed-upon time. Most of the time we walked alone. The protocol consisted of walking for ten minutes, stopping, making a series of four hoots that mimicked the Mexican spotted owl (four olés rather than five) or the calls of other species, and then listening. Silly as it might sound, it actually worked.

When we did hear an owl, we'd attempt to triangulate a location and get closer to it. The spotted owl is quite naturally curious. Sometimes we were able to get a confirmed spotting. Then, the following night, we'd go out en masse to try to locate and maybe capture one or a pair. This involved using mice or rats as bait, casting a net around the bird, then sexing, weighing, prodding, taking blood samples, and radio collaring (actually radio winging, as owls lack necks for collars). Only by giving the birds these unwanted baubles and using the receivers in radio telemetry could certain critical aspects of spotted owl behavior be studied.

Dark-eyed, docile, cuddly even, the Mexican spotted owls seemed peaceful and peace loving, but they are professional killers. Their mien is nothing like the larger, more fierce-looking, and much more common great horned owl. They had little fear of humans.

You'd get used to some of the sounds of the forest at night. At dusk the nighthawks would appear, carving circles in the darkening air and alternating between blips and an eerie kind of guttural groan. Bats would swoop around and creep you out by nearly touching you. The most common bird was the poorwill, with its inane dovelike all-night-long eponymous chants.

Actually, cattle were the worst part. You'd hear them long before you'd see them, tramping through the woods, and this always seemed to be in the middle of black bear country, giving grounds for fear or consternation. Cows might moo stupidly or forlornly, but the range bulls were more of a problem, as some of them would growl deep and ursine and exhibit threatening, earth-hoofing, bullish ways, and it was easy to mistake bull for bear.

Using headlamps and flashlights, you'd often see wide-set bovine eyes reflecting the beam. You'd frequently hear coyotes, close or farther off, as well as great horned owls and other, unrecognizable voices. The whole effect was unsettling, as though the forest had eyes. I felt the wilderness watching.

Setting out at dusk and going into the night went so far against the grain that I never really got used to it. All my training and all my experience taught me to be down off the climb or finished with the ski run by dark, not the reverse. My night vision has never been very good either. Although I never got hopelessly lost, I spent a lot of time alone. The most notorious routes were actually on the west side of Thousand Lake Mountain. Only veterans got these, and they always had bear stories.

The surveys revealed the diverse adaptation of the southern variety. The Mexican spotted owl, at least in this area, tended to nest and roost in the narrow sandstone canyons—in Douglas fir, ponderosa, or pinyon and even on ledges. They foraged up higher in the forest. This proved to be the opposite of what might have been expected. Although forage area was important, from a management point of view it wasn't strictly necessary to prevent logging on forage grounds. Unlike in the Pacific Northwest, these spotted owls held no great threat for loggers.

ii.

On Tuesday my companion is a hirsute Wayne County native named Blondie. Born in Caineville, Blondie spent her puphood on a ranch near Teasdale. A Chesapeake with an eighth of golden retriever, Blondie was named (by her previous owner) for her light coat. On the ranch Blondie's main job was to keep cows out of the yard. Although not the brightest minister in the canine kingdom, she has taken this job to heart and remains fiercely territorial. As we drive toward Loa, the county seat, from the back of the truck Blondie barks at every horse, mule, llama, truck, tractor, fence, irrigation ditch, cow, barn, sheep, emu, and goat we pass. Nearing the Loa drive-in, she lets go with a battery of barks certain to keep all livestock at bay. L . . . O . . . A . . . Love-on-Arrival. Love-One-Another. Love-Only-Animals.

Blondie and I have decided to turn our backs on Boulder. We could spend an entire week just exploring its north slope, but why start now? There's something oppressive in all that size. We've decided, instead, to assay the plateaus and peaks that surround Fish Lake, protuberances that can be managed in three-quarters of a day, and to return to our kennel at night.

The good people of Wayne County, hard-working Mormons for the most part, sometimes seem to lack a sense of humor, a sense their ancestors apparently had. Take Loa, for instance. It was named by Mormon missionaries returning from the Sandwich Isles, for whom the evidence of volcanism proved keenly reminiscent of Mauna Loa. But really. Mauna Loa? *Mauna Loa, Kiki Bobo! Mauna Kea, Kiki Nene!* Brothers and sisters, where are the palms? Where can be heard the pounding of the surf, 7,000 feet high? Is that Don Ho over there, or just Elder J. Mustang Taylor? Where shake the lovely girls in grass skirts? At the bank, market, or lumber store? There shake they not. Do the local inhabitants greet the visitor with a pit-roasted pig, a plate of poi, and a fresh, fragrant lei?

Not usually. Folks, this ain't no Blue Hawaii.

A few hours later, having left most of that Lovetown chatter below, having strolled up steep dewy meadows and startled cows, having trod the long summit ridge on every-colored rocks, Blondie and I find a tangle of guy wires, radio transmitters, repeaters, receivers, and dozens of useless car batteries of uncertain origin littering the summit of Mt. Terrell. These are obviously not remnants of the Fremont Culture. Perhaps feeling territorial, someone has etched a little note on a metal "Do Not Disturb—U.S. Government Property" sign: "ForeST SeRVicE, cLean uP YOUr GarBAGe!!!" Also on the summit tundra stand a few rock shelters, probably of Boy Scout origin. So much for escaping the trappings of civilization.

Three prairie falcons follow us down Terrell's summit ridge, swooping over us at 100 feet. I'm worried about Blondie, since she would be the tenderer morsel. I've been dive-bombed by birds before. We pick up our pace. We must be trespassing at a nesting area, though there are neither cliffs nor trees nearby. Perhaps the birds are pissed off about all the litter on the summit and want to hold us accountable.

The trio of birds eventually leaves us alone, swoops west, covers the UM Valley in a minute, and carves the air around the top of Mt. Marvine.

—

On Marvine's summit I find a register that contains the name and story of icy blues aficionado Frosty Tinker. Frosty Tinker climbed Mt. Marvine as an adolescent while staying at K's Kamp in Koosharem. He returned from California twenty-five years later to repeat the feat. One does not know whether Frosty was his given handle or rather an invented appellation, but surely life isn't easy if your name is Frosty Tinker.

One would like to ask Frosty whether this aspen-girt corner of the world seemed all that different after twenty-five years. The mountain could have been in an entirely different season on his return, obscured by memory to begin with, and perhaps enfolded in a July drizzle or August cloud or shining pretty as tomorrow in mid-September. A different place. As he plodded up the long curving meadows below or the talus above, maybe he thought of his dead parents, bad business decisions, marital misadventures, or the child he loved. Maybe he wondered how he had ended up in California, or why the aspen didn't grow on the slopes beneath the red-gray cliffs, or what killed the five cows that remained as skeletons, and why there would be so many cows unkilled, or how it would be to ski down such a long curving meadow, and if life could go on past that, and what was the name of that blue flower, that yellow one. His record indicates that he made the second ascent alone. At his side and at his back he would have sensed the loyal companion of physical deterioration. True, the exact pain of ascending is forgotten after twenty-five years, but revisiting the effort—the sweat and hard breathing and recalcitrant, unused muscles—it might have made Frosty Tinker reflect and wonder.

On mountain I am nothing. I do not climb mountain. Mountain climbs me.

Frosty Tinker never climbs the same mountain twice.

—

Looking farther back, in the great moving and shaking known as the Laramide Orogeny, this western side of the Colorado Plateau was heaved up in a vast flexure. As the Tushar Range formed further west and opened massive cracks and fissures, mammoth lava flows crossed this eastward land, covering the existing sedimentary layer cake with an igneous frosting.

Recent ice ages gave the land its present form. Because of underlying topography, the influence of prevailing northerlies and westerlies, proximity to ancient Lake Bonneville, and for a dozen other microclimatic reasons, the northern sector of the plateau semicircle received more snow over the millennia and gathered still more in glaciers, and therefore contains forms more truly mountainous. Mt. Marvine boasts the classic Matterhorn form. Tidwell Canyons display a textbook U-shaped valley. Terrell and Hilgaard sport gnarlacious northeast slopes and cirques. Moraines are scattered abundantly, along with drumlins, eskers, and a thousand pothole ponds. Even among the flat tops, it is an odd combination—glaciated lava—fire and ice.

As the Pleistocene glaciers retreated up the slopes, the spruce and fir forests followed. Today this Hudsonian forest remains only on plateau tops and below the rims as reminders, remnants, relics of cool blue 10,000 feet high.

—

Blondie is in back, Brother Otis is on the tape player, Sister Ruth is on deck. We drive up-county in early morning. One direction makes me wonder about this obsession with escape and hills, hiding, running away day after day. Maybe it would be wise to dig a few postholes or paint the damned trim. The better direction says when you get the mojo workin', you work it.

Something vaguely comforting abides in the blues. Both structure and rhythm are inevitable. The shuffle is the human heartbeat writ large. Whatever the chord or note, the blues begins and ends in the same place, whether upscale or down, and it's often rendered in sevenths, an unfinished, incomplete, slightly dissonant chord that underscores great longing. Sister Ruth finishes it with phrases of worn-out love that hint at completion but still leave it undone.

On Windstorm Peak the blues is painted all in minor chords today, played lefty because it's screwy, and tougher, and hell if you're born that way. Blondie feels it too.

—

A few decades ago a local bluesman, Lorenzo Larsen, began leaving his mark on the country. Something of a megalomaniac, probably of pioneer stock, certainly a Mormon, and undoubtedly a stockman, Lorenzo Larsen first took to signing trees, writing on aspen. All over this country, fancy Lorenzo Larsen signatures can be found, accompanied by the signatory year, LLs by the dozens.

There is a certain moxied hubris in the act—slicing tender tree flesh with sharp metal. But today we are forced to ask: *Lorenzo, just who in this great blue world do you happen to think you are?*

Sorry? Maybe it was more than territorial, the taking of trophy. Unwilling to confront the loneliness without a trace, he had to justify himself with these aggrandizement tattoos. Maybe not.

It got worse. Lorenzo moved on to leaving longer-lasting monuments: piles of rocks, cairns. Certainly his early cairning would have served a useful purpose—to mark a route through a canyon or over to a spring, but it was also a gateway to megalomania. As time passed he spent more time on it, elaborated on it, noodled with it, and shaped his cairns into likenesses of animals. For instance, on the ridgeline above the main road into Fish Lake can be found many members of a menagerie, crude representations of lions, tigers, falcons, eagles, and bears. Also a mini Stonehenge.

Beyond the swink, you embellish. This much Lorenzo Larsen knew. Life is difficult, let us grant, and we are often lonely. Let's imagine that Lorenzo was given to visions in copses of loveliest aspen, that he felt the spirit so strongly that he had to leave his relics, his spoor, this Mormon Druid, to say with signed trees and piles of rocks, "I am. I was here and that I was here matters. Let me show it to you. My rock piles will surely outlast me. Each time I etch my name in a tree or heap up boulders it is an affirmation and holy desecration in this my temple, my landscape."

Maybe it all just got away from him.

—

Plays heavy riff.

Cheering, applause, and whistling.

—

Halfway up a hill, any hill,
everything changes when you find yourself
halfway up, which is halfway to the top,
and three-quarters of the way
from the end of the journey,
from the end of the journey.

—

The whistling bugles of rutting elk fill the high register on a morning ascent of Mt. Hilgaard. Clouds hang far below in the desert, hiding the infernal land. Solomon's Temple, Cathedral Valley, Cedar Mountain, Moroni Slopes, Mussentuchit—all their Entrada pink is obscured. Seventy miles away the San Rafael is lost in the soup; only a few temples and spires rise above it. A chilly breeze blows on the summit, waving the elk grass, the stunted trees, the clumps of hardy krumholz.

Feeling the cool, Blondie and I chill among purple boulder fields on the western side, where raspberries and gooseberries hang ripe, perfect, bittersweet. Blondie chases squirrels. The lighter wind stirs the yellowing aspen leaves.

The tune is played throughout south-central Utah. The plateau stands cool and blue, two miles high, dark source of timber, grazing, water. Meanwhile, the desert below swelters in reds and oranges. The contrast works in winter too.

On skis, on Boulder, you glide amid dark spruce and naked aspen and gaze down Oak Creek at rocks red as embers, wild and twisted in their warm-looking remove.

Sometimes you look down on clouds.

—

The way up Hen's Hole Peak proves long and windy, and the way down is scary. It's not just because of the steep scree. You wanna talk about a dark wood? Blondie and I hurry through the Country of the Bear, black bear country to be sure, very active-looking bear country. The signs are everywhere—clear as lovers' names on a trailside aspen, the advertising of 100 marred trees, scratches that say, "This here's mine." *Fine, Mr. Bear, you go ahead and scratch your claim. No quarrels here.* Given Blondie's penchant for bolting after deer, I try to keep her close, since deer can lead to bear.

We lose our way. The trees close in, thick and blue, and we're being watched. We hear things. Just trees groaning in the wind? Bears? Heart-attack grouse? The muddy waters of the Mississippi flowing to the sea.

—

The tracks we follow
cattle, elk, deer, bear,
and all the scurrying rodents
that follow us.

—

The following year the same shoulder we traversed was struck by lightning, and Hen's Hole smoked through the summer and into the fall, smoked and smoldered till snow fell straight and thick and feathery.

—

And what of Frosty Tinker? He left us far fewer clues than Lorenzo Larsen—only two signatures and a few lines twenty-five years apart. We can speculate that at some time during the return it was easier to continue than to turn back. At some point turning back was out of the question. Maybe there was nothing to it. Frosty had stayed in shape by eating "nut cutlets and green leafy vegetables" and practiced yoga and trained for weeks and allowed sufficient time for acclimatization and he had taken young lovers and retired early and traveled the world on a vision quest, or he came back here on the way to somewhere else, to return to a starting point, a place with a tug, no room but some view, all this to feel the painful joy of it.

The standards can be happy or sad, and the best hint at both. "Let the Good Times Roll" mingles with "The Thrill Is Gone." The sky sometimes cries on a sunny day, backed with organ or horns. Red and blue make purple. The beat pulls you forward when you've got your head in the past. "Me, I got me a woman, but she's 200 miles away. All I got right now is this dog and a pair of worn-out boots."

I guess I'll find no love on arrival at my castle tonight, and this is the world's most beautiful place. Twelve bars. Twelve times twelve. Repeat. Passing over, passing through. Notes piled into measures piled one on another, steps and shuffles that become a song.

—

Wipeout.

The Mighty Blizzard of 1995

WHO IS STILL AROUND TO REMEMBER the last time it snowed thirty inches at Fruita? In one storm? Was it twenty-five years ago? Fifty years? The famous storms of 1949? Never?

The old-timers are gone now, the handful that lived in Fruita in the days before it became a national park, before the Park Service tore down the lodge, the gas station, many barns, corrals, and houses, and planted all these damned orchards. Lord knows it's more difficult to preach heritage, pioneer this-and-that with the houses razed, the natives resettled.

Today this snowy domain belongs to me. The only other person I've seen is a park cop, slowly making the rounds and protecting visitors by killing time, checking the toilet paper supply in the empty campground restrooms, and making sure no one speeds on the icy roads or leaves behind anything but footprints: climbing leaves sky-blue postholes in deep snow.

From this high vantage point the campground deer appear the same size as the barbeque grills, and the snow that covers slopes of river-rounded rocks looks like bubbles in the eddy of a stream. Walker Peak, Navajo Knobs, the Egyptian Wall—familiar landmarks—seem buffer now in contrast, more blushing red, deeper than backdrop, with the frosting.

All this to stand grateful for the solitude, a diamond-rare chance to wallow through thigh-deep drifts at the end of a January day, while a five-eighths moon rises over rim rock against a too-blue cold sky, and no distractions: no canyon wrens or spiny hop sage or Winnebagos, only a mirage of too-much fluff, a gift with a short life under the sun, and lonely breath in little clouds at the mouth of Cohab Canyon.

Drowning

I think the knowledge came to him at last—only at the very last. But the wilderness had found him out early, and had taken on him a terrible vengeance for the fantastic invasion. I think it had whispered to him things about himself which he did not know, things of which he had no conception till he took counsel with this great solitude—and the whisper had proved irresistibly fascinating.

—Joseph Conrad, *Heart of Darkness*, 1902

1.

I used to go out to Beas Lewis Flat to interrogate the trees. Sometimes I went there out to lunch. Partly it was an excuse for aimless walking. In aimless walking you can be open to whatever demands attention: trees, rocks, rodent tracks, clouds, a low-flying falcon, the spray spot of a cougar. The wind furnishes your aim. A desert wash nearly always goes somewhere. The things you find make your tale.

My eyes were drawn to the twisted-up pinyon and juniper trees, though, being living things and having souls, and standing singly without benefit of forest. Each one was different and each one had a story: twists and turns, droughts and seasons of plenty, tall trees of the pygmy forest. Beneath each was a shadowy mulch of cones or berries and needles. On many a rust-ochre slope there was no grass, or nearly no grass, but trees. The barren enduring strength of them led to Zarathustra moments: God is dead, everything is allowed.

Don't get me wrong. God was everywhere, but just past the city limits, beyond the edge of town, when the reddened landscape started its downward trend, *their* God no longer held sway. That toehold God had been overthrown as unneeded, replaced by demigods and goddesses, nymphs and fauns, voices in the breeze, voices in the trees. Replaced with windswept possibilities where every dearth was filled with life and everything was permitted.

It was Kurtz's jungle out there, too, because once you touched it, you could bring it back to town with you. It was always there to take if you wanted it, but you had to listen to the trees. Those trees spoke and some of them shouted. You only had to have the ears to hear them.

"Well, that's certainly interesting, Kevin. And tell me, how long have you been hearing these particular voices?"

Whatever. You hear them or you don't. Old roads tell stories. A granary or storage cyst salted away under an overhang testifies. A spear point or arrowhead or scraper or metate or mano has things to say. So does an antique singletree harness or an old boot in a pack rat midden or the lid to a jar or a shard of blue glass or any of the other elements of material culture. Records of passage, of passing through.

Surveying the landscape memory middens brings to mind the lawbreakers who came this way, the last semicivilized jumping-off point for the Outlaw Trail. Not the Hollywood type of outlaws, of course, but rather American peasants who turned their back on the regulated life and rode through Good Water and down through these breaks on the way to Robbers Roost, to freedom on the lam. They'd screen themselves behind cedars and ride down red-brown arroyos and no one needed to know. They left what they'd done back there. Up on the rim rock was tomorrow. But they had to keep their heads. If they messed up, there was no one to blame but themselves. And, yes, outside the law and order, the stakes rose high indeed: white-blue domes in a cold wintry sky. What there was to lose made them jumpy in the morning and edgy at night, made them careful, coyotes.

The question then became personal: how far can you go along that edge, along that ledge before you reach a point where you've no choice but to backtrack or jump? And if you chose to jump, there's no telling how far the next ledge would go before it, too, pinched in or spat you out in the crumbling slopes of other possibilities. You could get lost, trapped, squeezed, killed.

On the other hand, the many different versions of Robert Leroy Parker of Circleville, also known as Butch Cassidy, are nearly all projections of a story's author, or a wish fulfillment pinned on someone else. Simple badness has to be more than what it was. There's not much room for further mythologizing, and also all the room in the world. Butch as Robin Hood. Butch as kind to children. Butch dying in Spokane. Butch as Elvis. Give him perfect hair and blue eyes, and he's got charisma, he's got method, he's a star. Whatever you do, don't make him a killer. Don't make him a thief. Make him good with animals. Chivalrous with ladies. Helpful to the indigent. Make him a butcher in Rock Springs. Make him lots of fun in a black hat, reenact with him, forget he's a lawbreaker. But show him smirking in the famous photograph from Fort Worth with the Wild Bunch and see a Mormon boy who went way too far bad to turn around.

Faced with a life of drudgery, of farm work and poverty, as well as the chance of eternal salvation, Robert Leroy chose rather to err on the side of thrills and sinfulness. Go to Circleville and you will see why. Mountains circle the puny village like iron collar shackles.

The outlaws who rode these breaks felt the freedom. It's a sparse jungle, a jungle with spaces in between, but a jungle just the same, and the trees will be witnesses, but witnesses that never tell of what they see to judge or jury. Outlaws like Charlie and Rains Lee of Torrey, and Emma Blackburn of righteous Bicknell, riding beyond the last fences, clattering down the breaks and washes, into iniquity, to liberty.

The hippies sensed this when they came to town in the 1970s. Here was a place where you could do your thing in peace and quiet: grow herbs, make macramé, play guitar, throw pots, build a house, or save the world. For many years it worked. *Out here on the periphery.* The hippies formed a clan. In time we were invited in. Picnics, parties, camping trips, firework displays, boating excursions—a lot of group activities offered to outsiders by no one else.

Above all, a lot of grapevine parties. Parties in Caineville, parties in Good Water, parties al fresco in between. Parties with the Good Water Bitches. Parties with the Good Water Bastards. Moonlit hikes. Thanksgiving on top of Cassidy Arch. Climbing Fern's Nipple, or Molly's. A party meant some sort of activity—meal, birthday, festival—and the allowance of altered states, but for many years it was just the small stuff: a little bit of this and a little bit of that. Going out to lunch for a few hours with something to swill to bring you back down. A community. A party pod. But then Crystal came in and messed it all up.

2

One time I ran into Bird over in Bicknell between the liquor store and the Aquarius Motel. He was flying high on his Goldwing, hitting hard on all six cylinders, fully revved to the red line. He said he was headed up to the Hogan for the view. We shared a moment, a cigarette. I could smell the vodka on his breath from five feet. He was way too fucked up to be riding on anything other than a little red wagon. But that's the way it happened. Sometimes you'll try nearly anything. Because you can try it straight and do it. But it's always more interesting to do it with this little other thing or two going on in your head. Motorcycles can be good that way. Motorcycles can be essential that way.

Who the hell wanted a Harley to advertise your presence to the world, or hurt your hands from the ridiculous rattle? That flatulent roar of Old Milwaukee? Much nicer the subtler Goldwing. More polite, genteel, civilized. The way it shifted smooth, running through the gears like a hot knife in lithium grease. Romp on it and feel the feedback from high-quality shocks and stuff. Rustle up the throttle and approach the gleaming edge of warp-speed fear.

The initial befuddlement held the big allure of the herb. Get past that and see what happened—things became more involved and involving even if you were just dumb. But Bird wasn't just smoking a couple of doobies this time. Granted, he might have had a pair stashed in his leathers, but here was a case of at least four strong substances, four strokes of intoxication, each playing off the others, some legal, some not: a real Neapolitan of meth-weed-coke-booze and a smoke, a genuine BLT with a slice of provolone, a grand slam of ups and downs, intensifiers and down-shifters. I could tell he was just jangly with it. On a Honda. A bloody fat man touring Honda with a faring and more power than most small cars, headed for higher than the Hogan. Way higher. Headed for escape terrain.

But whatever. There's only so much a person can do to help someone who won't take it. Who needed help? Not him, not me. But when it comes to a betrayal, there can be all of this and so much more. Hands grasp the shovels so easily.

A betrayal needs three things in the following order: an offense, real or imagined, a conspiracy of othering, and a denial.

The plotting can be organic or planned, and both can work effectively, depending on circumstances or need. Let's look at the case more closely now. Let's say Bird committed a serious transgression while "watching" his kids, aged barely three and five. The two kids had wandered down the lane from Bird's casa and over to Owens's establishment, his good/old/best friend, Owens's establishment, the Arm and Leg General Store, which did hold irresistible allure: the flashing lights, the promise of candy or ice cream. The two unescorted kids had walked past an open, flowing canal and crossed what can be a very busy street, actually a highway, though the traffic really does slow down most of the time. Maybe some elderly Americans had helped the cute tots cross, or some Euros on holiday, so really, they probably weren't in any real danger—though it's very hard to say that with a straight face—because, generally speaking, watching one's kids involves a little more vigilance than letting them cross a highway. But anyway, let's say this incident occurred just after some of Bird's run-ins with the law, because impaired driving is a hobby and pastime and vocation among the hippies of Wayne County, and nobody's damned business until somebody gets popped by John Justice or rolls it while out and about. Let's further contemplate that Bird's old lady, Anna, had moved out, taking the kids, and she had also said some very rough things about Bird and his ways *while she was leaving, at the very moment she was leaving.* Let's say that a lot of things were said, and the reaction to the things was hateful and ugly, that objects were airborne, and plates and cups may have been broken and threats might have been made. And neither Bird nor Anna was really listening to what the other had shouted at that point.

After a resolution and vows to try work it out for the sake of the kids, Anna had dutifully dropped them off for the day, because Bird liked to play at being a good daddy, and they were trying to work things out, better than all the shouting. And the kids had left the house. They had wandered to the Arm and Leg. That left the next move up to Owens.

The kids were safe. They had been given candy. They could be occupied until Owens could call Bird and say, "Hey, moron, come and get your kids."

Now, unfortunately for Bird, the next move belonged exclusively to Owens. Owens and Bird had been friends since elementary school. Owens and Bird went back, way back. Owens and Bird had a magpie nest of history. Whom did he call?

Owens called the authorities.

Denial is the nautilus shell, a logarithmic spiral that hides itself within its own sense of invulnerability. It circles upon itself and grows in the dark places of the day-to-day. It can pull back and push out its tentacles. But gastropods have no hearing whatsoever. They must rely on vibrations.

Denial = Denali, the Great One. The High One.

A first chamber would be to deny that any of this was a big deal. A second one involved some elaborate and ridiculous excuses such as *I was just trying to let my kids learn how to do things by themselves—you know, to solve problems, be independent, no biggie.* Third comprised the belief that Owens hadn't actually done what he had so plainly done; friends don't do that to friends. Fourth: Anna Lee knew he was a good dad. Anyone could see that. Fifth: the civil authority of Wayne County wouldn't, *you know*, actually press charges or make any undue charade, demand a hearing, file a complaint, file another complaint, ask for witnesses, evidence, affidavits. Sixth: that representing oneself in such a circumstance and holding fast to (1) and (2) above would win the day. People are reasonable, *you know.*

Add to this other layers until you have a regular baklava. Prepare pine nuts and phyllo dough, honey. Bake at 350 degrees for several weeks.

3.

Crystal . . . Oh yes, Crystal. Pot made you stupid, but that was okay. Stupid was better than same. Stupid worked in many circumstances. *I think I'm dumb, or maybe I'm just happy.* Or maybe I'm just sampling the buffet. Just browsing. Out to lunch again. Stuff your nose with cocaine and you'd talk about yourself too much, smoke-a-lot-of-cigarettes, and spend all your money. Acid was great but it lasted too long and you never knew thumbs up or thumbs down. Mushrooms were the best but hard to find. The ones that grew on the mountains 'round here weren't strong enough. Speed made you introverted and jumpy, and after a while withdrawn and scared. Heroin was hard to get and hard to get away from. Crystal was the rainbow with claws. Crystal was all of these and more. Crystal was all of this and nothing. People paid attention when Crystal came around.

In the '90s and into the millennium Crystal Meth became the scourge of rural areas. You could cook it up yourself or you knew someone who did. It wasn't tricky to grow or time intensive. It didn't come from Columbia or Afghanistan. And it was cheap. Get started on some really good clean stuff, the medical-grade brown-eyed cousin MDMA, *ecstasy*, then mornings and afternoons and evenings just weren't the same after that. Your jaws hurt from the laughter. Arms sore from the hugging. You could embrace yourself and all others with your love, love, love.

But the hippies didn't stop at midnight and drive their minivans home. Nope, midnight was when things got fully fired up and amping. You could just stay up all night long with Crystal, all night, for days, for nights and for days, and then those crazy night birds started to wheel over town throwing sparks in the dark, and then they started to circle or maybe land on the deck and stare at you, and they too wanted to party with Miss Crystal, stare with those dark beady bird eyes, dangerbird. And when everyone knew it was you, when it was you, and when your old friends seemed no longer to be around or to know you, or know you, and when there just wasn't enough of the good stuff anymore, just this rancid battery-acid shit, and it would smell, and you would smell, scrape it out and scrape it up, and scrape. But then the drought would be over and your special friend would get some more, and you get some more, your special friend, and pretty soon you didn't know who knew, or what was who, or who was who, or who was Hugh, or Hugh was you, only that you needed it and more of it. And you knew they were coming, and they were coming, and so you locked all your doors and got your knives out and turned off all the lights and sat in a corner ready, and this is exactly because right at this moment they are coming, they are coming now, they must be coming now, and you sat there all night except when you had to load up another one and then another one and then another one after that, and that lasted for a few hours until you got the dosage right and beat it back with whiskey or brandy or vodka and something, and then it was time to turn on the TV and turn up the radio and flip on all the lights, with loud electrical silence, and crowded in a lonely room, and lonely in a crowded room, and the cigarettes gathered in deep piles, and maybe you need another one, and how many more packs or cartons do I have 'cause I sure as hell don't want to go out there to get another one, not even to the fridge, or where is my car, my car, and who took my car, and who has taken my car, and where is that large automobile, and who is watching me, and it went on like that with Crystal and on like that with Crystal and on . . .

So when the law enforcement officials of Wayne County caught wind that there was a whole lot of tweaking going on among the hippies, they used many ways and means to control it. In a small town or a sparsely populated county, it's not hard to work deals and to get to know anyone's business, because every speed stop and every DUI is leverage, and desperate leads to deals. The highest bidders decreed that you make sure the cookers and the users will be taken down.

Sometimes she made you so stupid with it, and brain-addled, and lovestruck that you'd fall into traps. And they'd get you.

I saw it work on Bird.

And I said, look, Bird, you can't trust anyone in this town. And I said, look, Bird, you've got the money so why don't you hire a decent lawyer to protect your sorry ass. And I said, look, Bird, you don't think they will, but they will. And look, Bird, the law don't mean shit around here, and the Constitution less, and if you represent yourself you'll only make yourself look like a fool. And I said, look, Bird, you know that Manny Lee and his sister, your former girlfriend/common-law wife Anna, are in a better position with the authorities, and she will make sure that she gets a good settlement on behalf of the children, your children, the two children that you had with her, the ones she took with her when she left, and she said some harsh things about you when she left, *at the very moment she was leaving*, you know, the ones you still see but whom Anna would love to take away. So keep your goddamned nose clean, and get out before it's too late, and don't think that what happened to —— —— won't happen to you—and worse—'cause at least he had an alibi and was innocent. And don't think they won't run you out of town, because when it comes right down to it, this is the wild Wild West, bro, and they don't like you and you are not like them. And they will run you out, and they will run you out—just for the sport, for the pleasure of watching you twist in the wind. And look, Bird, and look—.

And they got him. And he played the fool all the way to the penal facility. And Anna Lee got a good settlement, to which she was entitled, a settlement for the two children.

And they took his house. And they took everything else, except for the cat turds in the basement and his watercolors on the wall. And they put him in stir.

Twenty years of hippie heyday went up in death rattle smoke. There were others, too. Several others. A community, a clan, lost for the teeth-grinding, jaw-clenching, gutter-born stimulant, with sprinkles.

In the old days you passed a joint or a jug of Carlo Rossi, and you shared what you had, but when Crystal came around you flaked her off and lit her up, by yourself and all alone with others, a private porno, the cherry coals glowing orange-red in the dark, dark hours before dawn. And then that was you in the cave and no one else.

Me, I just watched it from the shore. I didn't want to get my feet wet and so shelled sunflower seeds and sang old sea shanties as the sun went down.

And Bird said, I might be drowning, toss me a lifeline.

And I said, okay, but why make it conditional?

And Bird said, what-the-Carlos, man? I might be drowning, toss me a lifeline.

And I said, glub glub glub. Get out of the water, my friend, my friend.

And Bird said, what water? Toss—. Hey, would you please toss me a—.

The element that's surrounding you, pal. It's always changing.

Oh, yes, I'm starting to feel it now.

Not ethereal and not elemental.

No, it's something like a wave. I can feel the current . . .

Get out of the water, my friend, my friend. And I said, get out of the water, my friend.

Get out of the water, my friend.

It was during this time that I stopped mingling with the Good Water hippies.

Part Three

South Wind from the West

MARCH ROARS. In the beginning there is the wind. Hours blow
into days of it. Ceaselessly screaming out of the west, hard steady
shaking at thirty-five miles per hour, gusting to fifty. A wind such
as uproots trees, flings corral gates open and shut like the ghost
of a long-dead homesteader, whips tree limbs so wildly that staring at a pocket orchard makes a person feel tipsy. A bloviation so
forceful that to drop anything that weighs less than a gallon of
milk . . . your hat, a box of cereal, a wrench . . . means kissing it
good-bye. Torn free and gone in a twirling flash, it will sail halfway
across south-central Utah before you can catch it.

Somewhere east of town, out on Beas Lewis Flat, is a place, a
boneyard, where all Good Water's missing tools, loaves of bread,
stray pets, cardboard boxes, and packets of seed can be found,
snagged by cedars or half buried in red earth.

To go outside is to face sure grit, certain misery. To hang laun-
dry gives a donation to tall cottonwoods. Hunkered down, some

reach for Baron Rothschild the Fifth for solace. March—a cruel time, a drying time—worse than the bottoms of December.

South winds are usually warm, but tricks of topography bend the winds destined for Good Water, turn them east, lift them up, cool them down, and then send them downhill redoubled. Bounded on the west by the two-mile-high Awapa Plateau, squeezed on north and south by two equally high flat-topped mountains, and edged on the east by low, infernal desert country that sucks, the village sits on a swatch of glaciofluvia, just begging to be blasted by any air on the move within 500 square miles. Good Water, an eye-blink town—all winds lead to it.

After days of fruitless blowing, the white stuff finally sails thick-flaked and horizontal. Yet there is no rest for the snow. Within an hour of falling it's on the move again, scouring down from the mountains, sailing through the pygmy forest, scooting across sandy flats, and winding into red canyons where it melts or simply disappears. Seated at a window you watch snow being torn from the dark flanks of the mountain. Tumbleweeds skitter across the airstrip like pursued deer. At sunset the blowing snow flows, an old gold wave, flooding the flats between Teasdale and Good Water.

J. Dwight Saunders, the landowner with the biggest spread in Wayne County, a plastic surgeon from the Golden State, a Republican, and a Mormon, bulldozed his tax-shelter bottom-land last fall in an attempt to control gum weed and sunflower. He succeeded in freeing up tons of his topsoil, red dirt that has sailed through town all winter long. By now a person would have thought that Saunders's supply of topsoil would have been exhausted, but that would underestimate the winds of March—winged plowshares.

Dirty Al Diaz lives in a ramshackle clutter of defunct trailers and eyesore sheds at the base of Dump Hill. Al is known for two things: his morning jog through town and his monstrosity of a fence. Mention Al and a townsperson will smile, "He likes the dump so well that he moved out there to be closer to it." And "Most people haul their junk *to* the dump, but Al built a fence *around* his."

To begin, there are stout posts sunk deep into rocky earth. These posts, laid out on a zigzag to provide strength against shear forces, are joined by 2 x 10 ponderosa planks. These planks are braced horizontally front and rear, and the corners of the fence are counterweighed with mudstone boulders.

Some say Al, a Vietnam vet, suffers from post-traumatic stress disorder, and that he dives for cover whenever a plane buzzes town. In point of fact, Dirty Al built his fence as the result of an unannounced visit from the sheriff of Wayne County, who found each of the following in his possession: a poached deer, a rustled calf, and a garden of tender marijuana plants. This hat trick sent Al over the mountain to stir in Sevier County, and thence to Gunnison. Our county jail couldn't hold so heinous a criminal.

First thing he did when he got out of the slammer was build his fence.

As an interesting sidelight, the same sheriff that popped Dirty Al was himself recently caught helping himself to game out of season while in his cups: a very fine pronghorn antelope and a golden eagle. When it was determined that a county sheriff's pastimes ought not to include poaching protected species while on the county payroll, and on the clock, not to mention the open containers strewn about the county pickup's cab, he was severely disciplined. He was fined a whopping $125, although he does face a tough fight for reelection.

It was generally believed that a wooden masterpiece such as Dirty Al's would last until the end of the world, but last night the northwest sector of the fence heaved and toppled. It remains buckled like a humongous spavined Hereford.

Most see it as an omen.

Meanwhile, the gales continue to rage. Saunders's dirt makes a midday curtain. Stockmen fear for their newborn lambs and calves and for the snowpack. A desperate line forms for the noon opening of the state liquor store in Bicknell. Night proves worse than day. The lucky few go to Mexico.

The ravens of town, on the other hand, denizens of the municipal garbage dump, have an easy time of it, clanking away the roaring hours under the big lee of Dump Hill, waiting for folks to provide them sustenance by dumping trash and rotten food over the brow.

If this howling ever stops, our ears will ring as though we had just stepped out of an AC/DC concert. Some calm day in distant May we'll make a pilgrimage to Beas Lewis Flat to retrieve some of the things lost and unaccounted for.

National Monuments

The Honorable William Jefferson Clinton
c/o The William J. Clinton Foundation
77 Water Street
New York, New York 10005

Dear Mr. President,

Thanks. Thanks so much for declaring this *muy grande* national monument down here in southern Utah in 1996. I know, I know, you did it for political reasons: to curry favor among the green votes on both coasts, the Hollywood elite, the liberal cabal, and you've never seen the area and probably never will, but who cares? You did it, and here's to you. You did the right thing. Did you ever!

This is why I think so. I'm fortunate enough to spend quite a bit of time down this way, and every time I drive over Boulder

Mountain and look down on your creation—not your creation strictly speaking, Mr. President, but rather God's—I just get goose bumps. I try to be in a position to toast you every time.

Sometimes in winter I ski to the top of Moron Hill, even higher than the highway, to get a raptor's-eye glimpse of all the grand country, and I know that everything I see before me is protected, locked up, exempted, declared, saved, and set aside— safe enough. Now, it's not entirely protected: there are still a large number of cows down here, and probably some people try to gather wood and camp illegally, and occasionally they don't always have the proper respect for natural processes, and it's well known that long-haired naked hippie backpackers can be found in the canyons occasionally, but still, it's protected *way* more than it used to be.

It's a National Monument, for goodness' sake, and the worst thing they can do is build a campground or visitor center, which they are doing, but there's not going to be a uranium mine in the middle of the Circle Cliffs or a coal mine on Fifty Mile Mountain or gas wells in the Moodys or a truck stop at the top of the Burr Switchbacks or a Pioneer Heritage Theme Park along Deer Creek or a motocross track in the Cheesebox or a marina at the mouth of the Escalante or any other mines in the Shinarump. No one is going to be able to build a lot of new roads or chain pinyon and juniper or drill or in general have unfettered license to rip-it-up, not without a grand struggle and heaps of red tape. This is a good thing, Mr. President, a very good thing.

It's a big, big, big, big, big area, Bill. Nearly as big as Yellowstone—85 percent of Yellowstone anyway, and you *have* been there, up in Wyoming, but the canyon country is just a little bit different. There aren't a lot of tall trees down here, or charismatic mega fauna such as bison, elk, moose, pronghorn, bear, wolf, and bambi, but there is a whole lot of space. Many people find the red rock wilderness just plain spectacular and sublime.

So here's my proposition, Mr. President. Next time you've got some free time, give me a jingle. I'd be happy to show you around Grand Staircase-Escalante National Monument. Now, I don't know the whole area, but I've got a few special places that I'd be happy to share with you. Don't worry. We don't need any special equipment. Just a decent truck, some food, water, and sunscreen. Maybe a cooler, a tent, some sleeping bags, and interns, but mainly just a little time. I've got plenty of gear to spare.

Given that the agenda of worthy deeds on behalf of your foundation surely takes most of your time, consider this as a fringe benefit: you could lose yourself, and it could change your world. The prophets went into the wilderness: Moses and Jesus and Muhammad. Muir and Gandhi and Abbey. You can find a new sense of scale in a windswept and colorful land.

In some ways it's a proper scale where *you* don't really add up to much. An added plus, nobody out there is going to tape your conversations or try to subpoena you. There's no e-mail and no phones and no faxes, no *Washington Post* or *New York Times* or Bill O'Reilly or Kenneth Starr or any of that excretory matter. You could leave your cell phone in the car along with the Blackberry. It's an okay to carry one for emergencies, but the wife and the kid won't bother you, I promise. And I bet we could ditch those flabby-assed Secret Service guys, too. Think about it. Give me a call . . .

Tell you this, Mr. President. I liked the way you did it—the way you made the declaration. I mean you and Bruce Babbitt and that Ickes fellow. What you did was use the Antiquities Act of 1906. You up and *invoked* it. You said, "This area is threatened by extractive industries; we're going to take it out of circulation." You had a little ceremony on the North Rim of the Grand Canyon in Arizona, and none of the national monument is in Arizona—that was a nice touch, but of course, Bruce Babbitt is from Arizona, so you up and invoked the Antiquities Act, held a ceremony, and did the deed in a neighboring state. That was a pretty great thing to do. You live elevated, man.

Now, all that business did seem like a slap in the face to many, many rural Utahans. It didn't make you exactly popular in these parts, and there were some who said harsh things about you, Mr. President, things that shouldn't be repeated. No, not real popular . . . but those good people weren't about to support you anyway, even if you gave out free grazing permits or ATV gun racks or commemorative .30-30s stenciled with choice bambi slaughter scenes.

You know that's sometimes the way things work out in politics: you win some, you lose some. There were a lot of people in southern Utah who didn't like what you did. They said a lot of *outsiders* had come in and told them what to do with *their* land. There's some truth to that, naturally. But you know what, it wasn't just outsiders. It really wasn't *their* land, either. It was, mostly, *everyone's* land, and we'd been dillying and dallying over what to do with it for a century. To speak frankly, there were some *insiders,* too, like Babbitt and that Ickes fellow, and also a little prodding from some Utahans—yes, Utahans.

When you waved your executive wand and changed history, there were a lot of people in these dusty little towns that said it would kill them and their way of life. But you know what, the opposite is true. Panguitch, Tropic, Cannonville, Henrieville, Escalante, Boulder—these places were, in fact, just about dead. Take a look at them today, ten-plus years after the fact, and they are thriving—thriving, I tell you. There are new motels and restaurants and stores and homes and paved roads and gift shops and places to buy genuine Indian moccasins and mugs with Kokopelli and calendars with eco-porn and DVDs and Grand Circle guidebooks and rubber tomahawks and postcards—and all of that just in the last ten years. For dying towns they sure look lively to me.

Now people from all over the world come to visit. Most of them just drive through on their way from Zion and Bryce to Capitol Reef. Most of them are just harmless sightseers in rental cars. Many are from Germany, Switzerland, France, Italy, Japan, North Carolina, and Ontario. Many of them stay in motels and eat in restaurants and buy lots of gifts for the folks back home. They take pictures. They enload a multitude of mega pixels. They stop at the visitor centers. They ask hard-to-understand questions. They ask stupid questions. "Who feeds the deer?" "Why are the rocks red?" They have a grand time.

Tourism isn't always great, sure, but it contributes far more in direct economic stimulus than running a few cattle on the public ranges or cutting down trees in the national forests. This is not just my opinion, either. It's well known. It's certified.

What strikes me about the whole process, Mr. President, is that some influential people told you what you should do and you did it. You liked the *idea* of wild lands, scenic beauty, preservation, that sort of thing. Wide-open spaces and red rock canyons might appeal to you, coming from Arkansas and living all those years in the District. That's something we've got a lot of in parts of the West, wild lands and scenic beauty, and places that should be protected as they are now: protected and enjoyed by lots of average people.

We had this writer out here named Wallace Stegner, and he used to talk about how the *idea* of wilderness was a good one and really important to all kinds of people, even to people who had never . . . or seldom . . . actually seen wilderness. The idea was vestigial from our frontier days, probably before that.

Wally liked to say that there were a lot of people who have never seen, say, the view from the southern end of Boulder Mountain or the eastern edge of Thousand Lake Mountain or the upper end of Long Canyon or practically anywhere along the Fifty Mile Mountain or the Hole-in-the-Rock roads, not to mention the Wolverine road or, shoot, even the Burr Trail and Notom Road, but they know that such views exist, and such views are marvelous, and such lands are vast and unsettled and undeveloped and quite wild. Knowing that there remain such lands in the modern world is comforting. Good for the sanity.

To be completely honest, I kind of like it both ways: knowing that such lands exist and knowing them more intimately, so to say. This is why I'd like to show you around, let you see firsthand what you did when you waved your executive wand, invoked the Antiquities Act, and set aside 1.9 million acres of country for the future.

And it's a good thing you did, too. Your successor, that imbecile from Texas, only sees land as useful for drilling. If you hadn't done what you did, there's no saying what we'd be looking at today. That Bush fellow has been really good for the oil and gas industry, but not at all good for the natural land.

So if you can make the time, Mr. President, I'd sure like to show you around. You really ought to come out to see these canyons and ledges and cliffs and ephemeral streams and canyons, arches and grabens and hoodoos and pour-offs and pinnacles and slots. You need to listen to the canyon wrens and coyotes and distant rumble of thunder . . . and the silence. But we will have to be careful. It just might change your life.

Very Truly Yours,
Kevin Holdsworth

In Loving Memory

THE GOOD WATER DUMP

THEY'VE FILLED IN THE FLESH PIT, hauled away three dozen old cars, and bulldozed tall piles of trash, rocks, lumber, and history. They've removed, flattened, leveled, tidied, smoothed, mitigated, and certified. And then they put a barbed wire fence and a U.S.-Government-Property Keep-the-Hell-Out sign around the old dump: all in the name of progress and environmental improvement. It's neither.

I spent many a productive hour at the old dump, looking for something useful and free, or playing at amateur archeology, and found a beat-up crib, a milking stanchion, dead pets, whiskey bottles, brand-new cards, a Park Service uniform, old dresses, busted chairs, shards of cheap china, pieces of broken mirrors, a cheesy conquistador lamp, rusted rakes, handle-less shovels, cement-coated hoes, worn-out boots, fleshy periodicals, crates of mushy vegetables, deer antlers, deer hides, deer heads, deer legs, tons of pretty rocks, old corral poles, tangled clumps of sheep fence, tires, bicycles, Barbie dolls, Christmas trees, books, record albums, and a boat. Some smart-ass left a fourteen-foot fishing boat out there for the taking, although it remained in perpetual high-desert dry dock, a few touches too holey for our reservoirs and lakes.

I was not alone in my magpie ways. Poor as the local economy was, there were always plenty of scavengers. Leave something behind, bring something home.

A balancing act: debits equal credits.

The dump was also a place for the three elements of rural fun: intoxicants, guns, and fire. Jeff "Stewmeat" Baker used to regularly come out to smoke a number, telling the wife he was "going to the dump," though the experience always uplifted him. You could swill all the Keystone you could stomach and toss your empties at the brow of Dump Hill, and the world would not be the worse for it. You could exercise your divinely inspired Second Amendment rights, blast away, and you were sure to bingo something out there; the associated brocade would dampen the ricochet. At night, if someone had brought in an old corral or some rotten cottonwoods or a few fresh pinyon straight off the range, it was a good place to light a little fire. A little fire that was sure to grow. And you could sit up in the cedars and watch it burn, and wait for the volunteer fire department to dive over from the Bridle N Bit and pretend to put it out.

Take that, EPA. Hell we can't burn our garbage!

No matter how blue you felt, a visit to the dump, except for the smell on a warm day, would make you feel better. With the wind at your back, the world at your feet, surveying all creation. Beyond the sea of refuse rose up red-yellow rim rock, the gap of the Fremont Gorge, the mighty bulge of Miner's Mountain, the crenellated top of the Waterpocket Fold; shoot, you could see all the way to the Henry Mountains. You knew it could be worse compared to your own personal disaster. At the flesh pit, it always was: ghastly and graphic, horses and dogs, goats and sheep, cows and cats in various stages of decay. Not for the faint of heart, but honest enough, *real,* sobering. That which awaits all of us. Dust to dust . . .

Now $96 a year buys a fancy black dumpster with wheels and a long blue turd of a truck to pick it up on Wednesdays. The new "sanitary landfill," twenty miles away, is so clean and tidy that even the ravens avoid it. No longer does a raucous unkindness fly over the flat late in the day. No more ravenous rawkety-rawk. And they sure didn't do an EIS to look at those environmental impacts.

Some see opportunity in the change. Pride of ownership looms: a new subdivision is being planned and platted right next to the old dumpsite. Eighty-five grand will buy two acres, a scattering of pinyons, an astounding view, and memories: a moiety of *nouveau* West to reinhabit.

This much "progress" probably can't last. Faced with the long, dull drive to Loa, the three-to-ten dollar sliding fee, the few-toothed dump keeper, folks will jettison their dead critters into any roadside ravine. Breezy as it is around here, just park your black dumpster on the windward side, and nature will take care of things, send things sailing east, somewhere else, somewhere new. Nothing ever really goes away. Not for long. Not in this country.

Bob's Truck

I'VE KNOWN BOB FOR TWENTY YEARS. He and Joanne have a rustic, homey, hand-built place in Grover, at the foot of darkly alluring Boulder Mountain. Grover's not much of a town. Along with their son Daniel, they comprise a significant minority of Grover's year-round population.

I've been on many hikes with Grover Bob as well as ski tours and fishing outings. I hired him to help enlarge the cabin, and we've never had anything in the way of simple disagreements, to say nothing of arguments. He seems a straightforward guy—what you see is what you get. It makes you wonder, though, how well you really know someone.

On TV they often interview the acquaintances of some psycho killer after he's been caught, and not one of the acquaintances had any inkling of their friend's deep dark side, his secret life, his awful ways and means.

Our culture recognizes gradations in the seriousness of crimes that depend mainly on intent. These range from cold-blooded premeditation (deadly serious) to negligent homicide (it's mainly your fault) to involuntary manslaughter (you tell your mama that you didn't mean to break that vase). Somebody has to pay.

Bob kept up the façade of law-abidingness by serving on the volunteer fire department, wearing the pager, attending trainings and brush-up courses, and going to meetings.

On years when the wood rats have been bad—and the Grovers live up in the pinyons—he would go to great lengths not to be cruel. He'd catch the wood rats in a Hav-a-Hart trap and then transport them six or eight miles up on Miner's Mountain to release them. Sometimes twenty a year. Quite a bit of trouble for a bunch of stupid rodents that love to build nests under the hood of one's automobile in the air filter housing. I don't think he even exercises his Deity-bestowed Second Amendment rights. Who would have known that there lurked in him the soulless heart of a killer?

—

Everyone who lives in the country comes in contact with the deer as they tenderly browse the pastures or spend their winters on sun-dried south-facing slopes or seek death along the highways and byways. Everyone who lives in the country has had close calls with the deer: close calls and not-so-close calls. Dead deer litter the roadways, with ravens scattering and golden eagles lifting off large and majestic.

Bob's truck, Whitey, was a Toyota. A nice little small-bodied, fuel-sipping, four-cylinder number. Cute, personable, and dependable as the wind. Whitey could hold lumber and tools for his trade, for in real life he pays the bills as Bob the Builder. He picked Whitey up secondhand and developed quite a soft spot for the death dealer.

I gave Bob a jingle a while back to get his take on the snow conditions. Joanne answered and said there just wasn't enough snow yet on Boulder, not enough for skiing, anyway, though the desert hiking had been good. She then told me that Bob might have to go to Grand Junction to get a truck. This was not good news.

"Oh, no," I said. "Did he hit another deer?"

"As a matter of fact," she said, "he did." She hesitated. "Here, you talk to him."

It turned out number five took care of that poor Toyota. Number five. *Uno, dos, tres, cuatro, cinco. Cinco*, ladies and gentlemen, five of the mule deer variety sent to meet their maker without provocation or a license. Five. That's the way you do it, Whitey.

Grover Bob started right in on with, "You know I wasn't going more than twenty, over on the road to Teasdale, and Danny was with me, and sure enough, that damned deer stepped right in front of us—at the bottom of the hill, and of course it was snowing really hard. I pushed on the brakes, but brakes aren't any good when it's snowing that hard on a road like that. I couldn't risk a spinout, so I laid on the horn but it was no good. I tried to swerve but I couldn't pull too hard. Then . . . Pow. Kablaam. Kathud. It was—. Well, it was messy, bashed in the whole front grille and cracked the windshield. . . . Meanwhile Whitey's bleeding out radiator fluid. And it's snowing, and Danny's there to see it. I had to call 911 because I knew I'd need a police report for the damned insurance. I got Carolyn Williams on the phone and she sent over the Coleman boys."

"Bob, you are a bad man," I said.

"Uh-huh. You know, the thing of it is—all this started four years ago. No, it wasn't; it was three. The first one was in 2002, February 2002."

"Five deer in three years?"

"I know. Can you believe it? But it was that truck—."

"Sure it was . . . Did you have to put it down?"

"Totaled it. You should've heard the insurance agent when I called. 'You again? Hey, Larry, it's the deer slayer on the line.' Ha ha ha. Ha ha ha ha ha. They took it away."

"Whitey'll probably try to tag another one on the way to Richfield."

"You know it will."

Who can explain it? Maybe it was because the truck had adorable doe-eyed headlights, a smiling and welcoming grille, a soft and gentle four-cylinder purr and ping, a powerful come-hither little-bambi attractant going on. The way things stood, Grover Bob and Whitey had racked up quite a tally.

"Three bucks and two does."

I said, "Next time you ought to get you a real Ummmerican truck with a big old brush guard in front."

"I know. Everyone at the road shed was laughing at me. 'Hell, what did you expect with that little Jap truck, Bob? You're lucky you didn't get killed.'"

"That's tough."

"Danny thinks maybe we could install an automatic kind of lift thing: hit the deer, scoop it up, send it over the top, plop it down in the bed, take it home, cut it up, air it out, and stick it in the freezer."

There was a long silence on the line. Not a bad idea, really.

Who can see into the dark recesses of a deer's heart? Why is it that they run toward you—right in the middle of a sunny day—seemingly bent on self-destruction? Perhaps in Bob's case the blithe bounding bambi chose their own ends, perhaps they saw the dashing doe-eyed white Toyota as an agent of deliverance. Bambi, don't fear the Reaper.

With humans we've learned to understand that some suffer from chemical imbalances that result in persistent gloomy feelings. Some of us inherit challenging disorders or suffer childhood trauma. We're taught to recognize the warning signs and to try to intervene before someone takes violent action, the first time often being a cry for help.

Deer at night is one thing, surely: when they stand blinded and frozen in the glare of headlight. But Grover Bob's m.o. was invariably to do them harm during the day. It makes you wonder.

"That was a darned good truck, too. It got thirty miles to the gallon. It hauled a lot of wood. It killed a lot of deer . . ."

As things turned out, Bob did get himself a new used truck, a sporty little blue one with 40,000 miles and not one dent on it.

Time will tell if it's Bob or Bob's truck who kills.

Is rehabilitation possible? Or will this be the story of a chronic repeat offender?

Some peck their marks in stone, some slice aspen trunks with sharp knives, and some spray-paint subway cars and freight trains.

Bob leaves his sign in mule deer desolation. In Wayne County, you'll know he's been around.

Clementine

YOU BUILD A HOUSE, YOU'RE GONNA LOVE THAT HOUSE. It can't be helped. It's like a child, you know. Its shortcomings you overlook. Its strengths you magnify. You cannot judge fairly. You overlook, you favor, you love.

I love my little house. She is my humble plain lady. One of my ladies. It is my heritage to have more than one lady. She is called Clementine. I have worked on her, enlarged her, built her from the ground up, made her more ample. Jennifer has worked and worked to make her more homey and inviting, hers and ours. Together. Our darling Clementine. It comes to this:

Shelter from the storm.
Pride, in the name of love.
Good cooking. The smell of good cooking.
A warm, dry place to sleep and awaken.
Shade.

A place to set and watch the sunset.
A bedroom for our son.
A place for the girls to fight over.
The source of something to do between times.
Before I had this house I wasted too much time.
She takes a lot of my time and plenty of my money.
Work the house and the house works you.
This edifice is rooted.
I was present when her roots went down. When holes were dug, yea
  verily, the mud mixed and blocks laid to root her.

The boy is old enough to help now, too. Together we have built fences.
  We hope to build more.
Grow trees in order to burn fires.
Burning fires is good coming and going.
Burning fields makes them greener. This the ancestors knew.
Fire can be used to drive game.
And used to cook the game thus driven.
I do not hunt for game but hunt.
Hunt for needing trophy.
Game? It's no game.
Hunt for safety, peace and shelter in this wooden cave. This is a cave
  for others, for all of us.

In the end it's planks or pyre.
This view is three clear hues, white, red, and blue. This is the view the
  house was built to view.
In viewing we take time to see.
In seeing we take time to think.
In thinking we can know.
Knowing we be.
By firelight and sunlight we enter the cosmos.
Rain river.
Wind winter.
Fire fall.
Rooted to earth every evening.
Mother mud mead magic, our darling Clementine.

The Hayrack

1.

AT ONE TIME I IMAGINED THAT THE DEMOLITION of the old hayrack would be a shaking off of ghosts—ghosts of those who built it and ghosts of what it was used for. Hayracks, also called hayricks, haven't been used with any regularity in agriculture for at least fifty years. In most areas it's been far longer than that, beyond the memory of an anachronism. The end of the nineteenth century saw the demise of most hayracks. In Wayne County the nineteenth century persisted until 1945.

Hayracks were used to transport threshed hay or grain from the field to the haystacks. A hayrack was composed of a brandreth, or framework of wood. The brandreth could be used either with wheels or as a sledge. A hayrack such as this one would have been pulled in sledge mode by a team of strong horses or a truck or tractor. It measured about ten feet across and twenty feet in length. It was not the sort of implement you carried around with you, so it spent its useful life in these fields and was put out to pasture here as well.

These days the job of cutting hay and cubing it for storage is done by expensive, loud, and wonderfully efficient machines. In the old days hand thrashing of hay and grain was done with the aid of a scythe. It is hard to imagine a more tedious job than scything some acres in alfalfa hay, lucerne, timothy, or wheatgrass.

To fully appreciate the power of manual labor, I suppose I should have cut the hayrack into pieces by hand, the way it was built, using a bow saw. Instead I used a chainsaw. Using one means confronting mortality. Chainsaws are good for slicing poles and trunks, also legs and femoral arteries. Their snarling menace can rack a careless person down at the undertaker. I put off demolishing the hayrack for some years after its time was due. I've owned five or six chainsaws and haven't liked any of them.

I'm not sure how many years the hayrack had laid fallow before I bought the place, but for all my years it provided a useful platform for setting things on and a great table-bench from which to watch the sunset. In the meantime, the planks were silvered and nearly rotted out, the wild currants grown up between cross pieces were tall and robust, and it was finally time for the old hayrack to go.

I imagined that recycling the hayrack would lead to moments of profound reflection. In reality it was pretty much a matter of long, hard, and sweaty work. Sixty- or seventy-year-old wood slices quite easily with a sharpened chainsaw, but the bolts, spikes, and nails, some hidden, dulled the chain, and it's awfully tedious to stop and sharpen it, so often I plunged on, forcing the nasty two-stroke motor to work its magic on sun-bleached gray logs and planking.

The real benefit of demolishing the hayrack manifested itself several months later, and it was a simple matter of fire. Fire against water. Heating fire.

To build a proper hayrack, you must know your wood. You must know where to get it and what it can do. There are three main types of conifers used for lumber in south-central Utah, and each is called "pine," though only one is.

Yellow "yellar" pine (ponderosa pine) will snap if you look at it wrong. It's heavy (ponderous), sappy, and often of various colors—yellow mainly but also often quite a bit of blue. Yellar pine works fine for siding and fences, and with the lovely streaks and scenes of blue, it makes gorgeous cabinets and furniture. Yellar pine has some considerable compressive strength, but it does not have much in the way of shear or resistance strength. Logs of it make serviceable cross members. It won't span much distance without failing, and it's relatively heavy.

White pine is actually either Engelmann spruce or subalpine fir. It is indeed white and it maintains limberness, such as it is, which is precisely what you don't want in the present circumstance. Workable and light, it's just not very stout: good for light planks, poor for cross members.

If you want a strong board (or log beam), you've got to turn to fir, Douglas fir, and you will travel far to find it in these mountains, farther still to fetch it, cut it, and carry it home. Doug fir is nearly always found near water but not in it. Red barked and majestic, up to 120 feet high in a good specimen, red pine is amazingly strong. How strong is it? No North American wood grows that is stronger.

Today there's no red pine within ten miles of this place, and there certainly wasn't much in the early days. No, to get you some red pine you'll need a good wagon, a few days, and someone to take care of your livestock while you're out trying not to break your neck while bringing home some coniferous bacon.

For the frame and skids you want red pine. But you don't want some forest monarch twelve stories high. No, you want a young robust tree, six or eight inches in diameter, and close enough to a track or trail that you can skid it down through the underbrush to your wagon. You'll know it when you see it. And when you see it you will rejoice. You may want to wait until the first two snows. Casting about for good beams can be a little like fishing. There's luck, dumb luck, and inspiration.

These are the three useful types of pine. The next one isn't treasured for its utility.

Near a place known as Happy Valley grows a congregation of bristlecone pines. Other small forests of bristlecones can be found on top of the Anthill and on the north side of the difficult-xto-reach Brown Benchmark peak. The bristlecone pine is the oldest or second-oldest terrestrial organism. Some bristlecones are four millennia old. In these parts, they have lived for centuries. When talking about the oldest bristlecone pines, some say that such trees were growing when Michelangelo unveiled his eighteen-foot giant in Piazza Signoria. Some grew when Donatello carved his more precious David of wood. Some grew when Jesus rode into Jerusalem on the back of a burro. Some were alive when Athens had its golden age. Indeed, some bristlecones now living were thriving when blind Homer recited his tale of men in skirts and swords clanging on the windy plains of Troy.

An infant bristlecone looks like most other conifers but with somewhat more needly bows. In youth, bristlecones form the most lovely Christmas tree: comely in symmetry, triangular shaped, rich with greenery. As the centuries pass, gnarlment sets in. Hoary bristlecones twist like Laocoön. In places their branches are barren, desiccated bones. An old bristlecone may have only the slightest hint of growth. They seem to be living with their own deaths but denying it with small ephemeral greenery.

With climatic change threatening all niche organisms, we will have to watch closely for the fate of the bristlecones. Like so many others, they may be forced into retreat. And if they cannot retreat to find a new niche, which they probably cannot, being elderly rooted, then three centuries of burning carbon may do what forty centuries could not do and eliminate the beauties.

2

This snow, too, is ephemeral. It was not here yesterday. It will not be here the day after tomorrow. But tonight, in the gloaming, while it falls steadily, it inches the field with just enough to ski upon. Few winter days yield skiing in the backyard. The opportunity is not to be missed. I couldn't talk Christopher into joining me, or Jennifer, so I'm making loops in the near dark, while the snow is falling. Each pass makes the trail a little more packed and slicker. Each compression wrings air out of the snow, replaces air with water. Inside, Jennifer and Christopher are warmed by the wood fire built from the old hayrack.

This old style of skiing, known as cross-country, originated in the lands of Scandinavia on skis made from wood—ash or spruce or alder.

To ski on one's field is throwback pleasure.

The hayrack transmutes in the firebox. Heat from that old hayrack wood that stood in the orchard for all those years. In fact, it stood before I planted the orchard. Dried, seasoned, used then stored, the wood burns clean and moderately hot.

The track grows faster with each pass.

The best fires come from a combination of wood fuels: a hardwood of some type—locust is good, or willow or elm or oak for heat and longevity; pine for pitch and easy ignition; aspen or cottonwood for even-tempered steadiness; juniper for its spark and bouquet. But life doesn't always present a precut and stacked woodpile. I should have more wood in the woodpile than I do. You make do.

I'm skiing in ovals in the dark. All is good in the world.

The ski never leaves permanent marks. To say you are an avid skier means that you practice your vocation on something that is not always there, that you leave no marks. Your efforts are illusory, ephemeral, not lasting. To ski in the backcountry, deep into the backcountry of the Rocky Mountains, you leave tracks that no one else will ever see, or at least there is the possibility of such a grand scale of remoteness, unwasted effort fleeting in its proof. Closer in there will be "glory lines" laid down to fluff up one's sense of pride, but they too will vanish in the next storm.

I suppose when I was younger there wasn't much I'd rather do than leave unlasting marks on remote white slopes in winter. Now it's enough to ski with wife and child.

The hayrack would have been conceived in terms of usefulness. It takes time to build something that is useful and will be for years, decades. If a piece breaks, fails. or wears out, it can be replaced. When technology changes, however, artifacts of the previous economy can become as useless as someone's rusty lawn ornaments down the line.

I believe that this house will outlast me. I believe it will outlast my children. I hope they will have children to share it with, to leave it to, but I have only five or ten or twenty or thirty years left under the sun. When my time comes, I hope to have no worry in that way. I worked here. It pleased me. I left my mark and left.

Going round and round: if at first I had no way of knowing what I was doing, and no real way of knowing that I couldn't really know that I didn't know what I was doing, that statement is both true and a reflection of then and now. I'm sure I didn't know—the proof is evident—but I'm equally sure I wouldn't know I didn't without the experience of knowing, of learning through trial and error. Epistemologically speaking, nothing works like attempts and failure, yet once taught the right way, persistence in error becomes both its proof and its chance for redemption.

To see yin and yang in all phenomena is merely to see what is, and in seeing what is, to see what is not. My birth kills me. My efforts deny my death.

Art is permutation of the fleeting into the concrete, the pinning down of desire.

At least that's how it seems, skiing in circles in thick-falling snow. The distant streetlights make cones in the mist, the video screen glows blue through the windows, the chimney pipe disgorges heat and light and smoke from many summers past.

In the morning I'll take another loop or two, but the sun is already at work on the scanty snow. What I packed last night will soon melt into the field, leaving no record of the passage of ski on snow.

3.

We ski leisurely up Carcass Creek the next afternoon. The clouds have lowered again and threaten snow. Critter tracks abound, marks of passing. Hares and squirrels and deer and wood rats. All kinds of birds. Carcass Creek also features a great many fine specimens of indigenous trees and lies at the right elevation to limn rich variety: pinyon, juniper, ponderosa pine, red birch, box elder, aspen, cottonwood, Doug fir, subalpine fir, and blue and Engelmann spruce. Each of these trees bears witness to both drought and plenty in its rings.

It is rare enough to ski at Carcass Creek that it should be done if possible. I brought Chris up here on my back at first, then we pulled him in a small red sled. Now he is catching on but still there's work to do. He *will* think it's a good way to spend an afternoon, Jennifer reminds him. He *will* enjoy this incredibly boring and old-fashioned family time.

Walking is fine but skiing is quieter. Skiing in a storm is quieter still. There is only the sound of our breathing and the soft scratch of ski on snow.

Maybe someday he'll tell his kids about skiing up Carcass Creek with his mama and papa.

I have wandered by myself and with my family. It is good to have companions. It is better to have affection. Bad as I am, my boy calls me Dad, the only one he'll know, and Jennifer calls me Mister, for she is a patient woman, and better than I am, and stronger. Our love forms a frame. Over the years we have stacked our own memories: the full moon rising over the Henry Mountains, the deep blue shimmer of Fish Lake and its pelicans. Walks in the canyons. All the places we like to visit and the ways in which we do. Some wander widely seeking adventure and newness, some wear out the pathways on home ground. Each year we fork another layer on the breadloafs in the pasture.

We drive slowly back to town as the snow falls big-flaked and hushy. At home the morning fire has grown cold. I stuff a few small pieces of hayrack into the stove, crumple newsprint into something like a snowball, light it, close the door, and open the damper full. Soon the fire is blazing. Rounds of summer grown on hillsides, felled and brought to town, racked and worked for years, then fallowed to wither and rot. Cut to length, this wooden record serves to keep us warm in winter idyll, and then the warmth is gone.

House Rules

A good hobby may be a solitary revolt against the common-place, or it may be the joint conspiracy of a congenial group . . . In either event it is a rebellion, and if a hopeless one, all the better.

ALDO LEOPOLD, *A SAND COUNTY ALMANAC*, 1949

WHAT TO DO WHEN THE WORK IS DONE? Or better yet, before it is started?

Hobbies are activities practiced in one's leisure time and on a consistent, regular basis. No Puritan, Aldo Leopold reminds us that leisure time is correlative of civilized life as opposed to civilization. "The man who cannot enjoy his leisure is ignorant, though his degrees exhaust the alphabet, and the man who does enjoy his leisure is to some extent educated, though he has never seen the inside of a school." Leopold adds artifact to his explication by pointing out that a hobby must have some sort of trophy, although we would add that the artifact does not have to be material—a thingy—it may be simply a memory.

Because Leopold comes to conservation with a rifle in hand, his distinction of trophy makes sense. He is more subtle than those who collect dead heads, though. A nicely mounted bull elk head and rack hanging on the dark-paneled wall of the singlewide next to the Miss Makita pinup poster and the Dogs Playing Poker scene done up in black velvet is only the most obvious kind of trophy. There are others.

Take fishing. An angler doesn't say, "I'm catching fish"; rather she says, "I'm going fishing." In some hobbies the journey makes the artifact. It is possible to have a successful day hunting or fishing or hill walking or bird-watching and bring back nothing for trophy. The mountaineer certainly seeks the summit as trophy, to say he has been there, but the mountaintop must be left behind. Trophy need not involve the shedding of blood. The hobby poet boasts fine lines as fruits of suffering. An open-air painter might hold up a canvas movingly smeared with pigment. Nobody gets hurt in stamp collecting, nor does the numismatist do any lasting harm.

A sport, on the other hand, whether team or individual, is an activity governed by rules, lines, traditions, and overseen by referees, umpires, judges, or the clock. There must be winners and losers. In sport, a trophy is given for winning. The contest has a set beginning and ending, and most modern sports are more competitive than leisurely.

A game is the third category of leisure-time activity. Scrabble, poker, pinochle, hangman, cribbage, bocce, bridge, croquet, charades, curling, golf—these are all games. A game is played mainly for enjoyment (golf would be the obvious exception), and a game is played primarily for the score. Most of these games don't require any special athletic skill, but one's ability may be enhanced by years of practice. Another feature of the game is that the deck may be reshuffled and dealt again: one can be both winner and loser in the same night, and often is.

I'm investigating these differences to see where horseshoes fits in. It shares something with the hobby. The practice of tossing curved hunks of metal forty feet at a metal stake is entirely useless. It is also a revolt against the commonplace, nobody's real line of work. Fun? Some of the happiest, most intensely pleasurable moments of my life have been idling away the hours, heaving shoes. Moments of deepest, darkest sorrow, too. These moments have been shared with friends, "the joint conspiracy of a congenial group."

My horseshoe trophy is the pits: two of them hacked and spaded deep into the sod on the eastward edge of the place. Twenty years ago I located the pits out of the way in a patch of lawny pasture with a very good view. In the meantime, the neighbor planted a row of windbreak cottonwoods and poplars that provide early-morning shade and the tinkling of leaves.

It took some time to learn how to take care of the trophy pits. Digging or tilling is not enough. To keep weeds from growing and the neighborhood cats from using them as a litter box, the pits are tarped when not in use. Because dirt is lost during normal tossing, it must be replaced. The native soil tends toward clay, so it's augmented with sand, and not just any sand but designer sand, Kevlar-reinforced, titanium-alloy, Italian leather, grade A fancy pure quartz sandblasting sand, several dollars an eighty-pound bag.

At the far end of each pit is the special gleaming trophy: rounded berms a foot and a half high. Useful to stop the shoe from skidding, these rise as heaped-up testaments to many hours invested in delicious idleness: grassy demi-knolls formed by the steady grounding of shoes: breakers crashing against the shore, sending up waves of sandy spray.

Our play is steeped in ritual. Before a match can properly begin, there is the requisite congeniality of preparing the pits, done by several players working together. Removing the tarps, pulling weeds, hoeing the surface according to personal preference—some like it deep, some like it springy—and pounding in the stakes. Music loud and mellow must be available. Swill is procured, the snack table set, sunscreen applied, moods altered, lawn chairs laid out for spectators, and warm-ups stretched until play finally commences. It will last for hours, sometimes for days.

Horseshoes has few rules and they are easy to learn. A ringer is worth three points, the rarer leaner two, and a shoe within the width of a shoe and the stake earns one, two two. The genius of the game is that only one player (or team) can score per frame, the closest one, so sometimes it's necessary to claim, speculate, debate, fibulate, threaten, and then measure to see who is nearest to the goal.

Penalties are rare but necessary to maintain the integrity of the game. No-nos include tossing shoes at opponents, stepping over the (ever-moving) imaginary line, moving a shoe that needs to be measured, or tossing blue if you are presently gray.

Based on much experience, it is possible to formulate the following Zen principles of horseshoes.

You might lose and often will.
You might win and sometimes do.
You will score points.
You will take points away.
You will have points taken away.
The mojo comes and goes.
It is good to toss first.
It is better to toss second.
Contest every point.
Measure when you must.
Always prepare the pits.

But none of these principles is enforceable, and horseshoes doesn't have any of the tedious, involved, or arcane rules of sports, or indeed of most games.

In keeping with the delights of a little harmless competition, it would be good to point out some of the other advantages horseshoes offers as leisure-time activity. It costs next to nothing.

Horseshoes do not increase one's carbon footprint. Playing burns a few calories and stretches some muscle groups. Equipment lasts for years, and all that is required for upkeep is the occasional filing of burrs and perhaps a coat of paint. There is no need to slavishly update equipment based on planned obsolescence or marketing hype. Injury is unlikely. Officiating has to be mutually agreeable. No special uniform is required, although some favor loud shirts and gaudy dresses for the psychological advantage bestowed. In keeping with the spirit of tribal gathering, a good day of matches features banqueting, periods of not playing, and trips to the woodshed. To play horseshoes you need no special gear, only beer.

It is good to win. The stakes are low enough, and in a good match, winning is possible only by doing harm to one's opponent, by playing defense—bettering or knocking out the opponent's shoe, which is a pleasure in itself and also because to win you must both score and defend.

A true connoisseur likes a close contest best. An occasional blowout gives only a sugary thrill. A seesaw battle surmounts. Strings of one-sided contests are for lowly spirited bullies and oil companies. Indeed, a come-from-behind victory may be sweetest.

People who actually make horseshoes into a serious sport— where winning is everything—are not welcome here. Those who train and practice, who toss ringers too regularly, who use performance-enhancing drugs can get on down the road. We play infrequently to make it better, and Good Water is the only place we play. Round here we're strictly amateurs, hobbyists. The reason horseshoes works well as a congenial group activity is that all are more or less equal in skill and lack thereof.

One of the most inexplicable things about horseshoes is the way it comes and goes: the mojo, the scoring, the habaneros. Again, we're talking amateurs here, not robots. A player may get hot and score on every toss, and maybe the heat will continue for a game or even—rarely—for an entire match, but inevitably he or she will go cold. And we're not talking crisp and bracing here, we're talking arctic. Sometimes the whole game goes cold—all four players tossing clunkers, bouncers, and bricks. Then someone will catch fire and it goes on and around again.

Speaking of advantages: horseshoes is a pursuit minimally affected by intoxication. A little of this and a little of that may even make a player more relaxed and toss better and lessen the sting of losing. "Well, one played poorly, surely, but at least there's more special bitter in the cooler to soften the sting, old chaps." And if a player takes the potables a little too far and becomes sloppy, what's the harm in that? It's hard to see how it could lead to injury or violent behavior, although the brush-back toss or sky-pilot shank might become more likely.

Psychology? The following are just a few of the things you can do to rattle an opponent. The most obvious is banging the shoes. On the brink of a super-serious point, it is nothing to strike the shoes together to create a clanging distraction. You can't do this often, so plan accordingly and ration the annoyance or risk a penalty. Other ways to ice an opponent include clearing the throat, coughing, receiving a cell phone call, dropping a shoe, a sudden burst of flatulence, an irrelevant question, popping a cold one, a loud sigh, the spotting of a sharp-shinned hawk over yonder or a bambi in the pasture, a query that begins, "Hey, do you remember that one time—" or asking, "Whose turn is it?"

People who bring their dogs should be treated with suspicion. Invariably Rover wanders into your view just as you're about to try to knock Rover's owner's leaner off the stake, destroying your concentration, so dogs, generally, should be tied up during important matches. Children, though more difficult to restrain, can be useful. They can be trained to inquire as to the score just at the crucial moment or, if the score is only too obvious, then questions about favorite colors, preferred makes of car, musical styles, have you ever been to Oklahoma? and so on may be used to great effect. Also, it's more subtle to signal a watching child to interrupt at the crucial moment than to train a dog to do it.

More collegial and psychologically damaging is the gentle put-down following a particularly bad toss.

"Friend, let me point out the pit for you. It's right here, about four feet by six feet."

"Actually, you try to hit the stake, not the pasture. What did it ever do to you?"

"Say, doesn't that new job of yours offer vision coverage? You might need to look into that benefit."

Speaking of trying to harm one's opponent, I used to play tennis—singles and doubles. Tennis is a very silly game. Doubles was always quite a bit more fun, especially mixed doubles, as it combined socializing with scenery. As anyone knows, the best strategy for winning at doubles is to hit a ball directly at whomever is playing closest to the net, trying, in effect, to do the person harm, but in a nice way. The opponent must react to imminent danger and protect him- or herself rather than return the ball.

I believe a similar thing happens in horseshoes with the threat of a brush-back fling. Big-souled players will compliment an opponent for a good toss, even a toss that does your team wrong. Lurking in the sand, though, is always that chance of the harm that you can do and can be done to you. One badly shanked toss throws down the gauntlet. *Whoops . . . Didn't mean to . . . Sorry . . .*

To avoid conflict, our house rules require switching teammates after each match. This way the person you just hated and wanted to die is suddenly your new hope and best friend in the world.

When a really bad toss heads your way, a good tension breaker is a highly dramatic and exaggerated get-out-of-the-way little jump thang. Don't hesitate, if the time is right, to do an all-out gallop away from the pit if a shanked toss comes too close. A well-timed Forrest Gump dash will also earn plaudits and guffaws. I have even employed a full-on James Brown faint when giving it my all after dodging a malevolent hurl.

Many of the finest hobbies, games, and sporting activities take place outside. There is something seedy about those televised poker tournaments with their greasy-haired, cologne-drenched enemy combatants in ghastly shirts and pimpy baseball caps. Outside in the big arena, conditions come into play: weather, wind, temperature, rodents, birds, lighting, lightning, etc. It's impossible to imagine a ski race happening indoors. Baseball provides a clearer example. Playing indoors on carpet in some gigantic stewpot named for a corporation is nothing like an ocean-breezed chilly October night at a genuine stadium.

One of the many shortcomings of NASCAR is that although it takes place outdoors, it appears actually to be indoors: the short oval track, the repetition, the cowboy music, the round and round, the olde-tyme religion, the Republicans, the fake headlights . . . Compare this toilet swirl to the exhilarating grandeur of road racing, Can-Am, Formula One, the twenty-four hours of Le Mans or Daytona, the back roads of Morocco: it's night and day.

As I was saying, horseshoes is played in the bracing open air. Indeed, it has been played in Good Water in the rain, in howling wind, past sunset and into the gloaming until you couldn't see a shoe in front of your face, and even in the snow.

Snow? I can describe but wish I could explain it.

Late February. A meeting of the high priests, a gathering of the clan. By noon the pits were prepared. Soon shoes and stakes were clanging. By late afternoon we tossed beneath a plummeting yellow-curdled sky. The wind blew warm, then less warm. Golden grasses rustled. All the leaves were brown and matted along the fence line.

At four p.m. the snow started sailing in from the west, wet and thick and feathery. Despite the snow, because of the snow, we played on through the twilight, flake-coated specters. All was white: us, the air, the ground—except the pits, divoted snow-free from the tossing. We tossed fast to keep it that way. We tossed until we could see no more.

Eventually we betook ourselves to the cabin. Inside we shared potables and viands and stoked the fire with locust and pinyon. Coats hung on the corner rack, drying. We played games of chance, banged drums, and talked about our feelings. We talked about the ones we loved and loved them more because they were not here. There were winners, there were losers. As we played, we cast interested glances outside to watch the snowy progress that continued, and as we took to our bedrolls, it progressed further still. Six or eight or ten inches gathered.

In the bluebird morning after the storm we dug out the pits, which was easy enough to do with the weightless frosty ice powder, scraped clear the launching pads, and simply played some more. When there was a disputed call, we marched the forty feet to confer, and when it came to that, we dug out a shaft of grass to use as micrometer as always, still debating, casting aspersions on each other's vision and intentions and character. We played until we had worn tracks on the white night-blown carpet. We packed the snow. We played in coats and hats, with gloves on. Playing kept us moving, kept us warm.

The Egyptian

IT WASN'T REALLY THAT LONG AFTER he beat his first serious morals charge that Landy Covers got the government-backed low-interest loan to build his motel, the Egyptian, currently the Wonderwall. Landy Covers was well connected. He was well connected because he ran the county road department. True, he wasn't from Wayne County, but his wife was, and he could sure talk the talk about the outsiders, about the Sahara Club, about the heavenly Second Amendment, about the goddamned SEWER (Southern Utah Wilderness Alliance) extremists and their penchant for suing. No, to most Landy's heart was in the right place, and what better way to give it to the outsiders than to be head of a county department. Building roads, claiming trails as roads, and bulldozing new roads was progress and progress was always good.

In those days, just over the hill in Garfield County the locals were giving the chip-sealed middle finger to Terry Martin and all those other tree-hugging, obstructionist, anti-everything-human, Subaru-driving, socialistic environmentals with the paving of the Burr Trail. Wayne County had nothing like that controversy but followed along and one-sided up with it.

When Landy applied for that low-interest loan to the Six County Association to build a motel, he got it. He did, and everybody said, *You bet, hell yes, Landy Covers can get that job did and bring in them turistas.*

The thing was, though he beat his first serious morals charge, there were rumors, and Landy had been given nicknames, nicknames suggestive of serious moral lapses, and they went round, but nobody ever had the huevos say them to his face.

I'm trying to explain this slice of history to Don Juan and D. Harry Menzies as the waitress refills our coffee. Harry does NEPA compliance work in Wasatch Front and has a second home in Good Water. As you recall, Don Juan works in the national park and lives in employee housing known as the Fishbowl.

The waitress is a good one and doesn't fear touching our coffee cups—believing, as some do, that it'll keep her out of the Celestial Kingdom—and pours readily even if we don't ask.

I'm delaying the Landy story just a bit to see if Don Juan asks for some grated cheddar on his scrambled eggs. Over the years I've had many breakfasts with Don Juan in several western states and invariably he asks for grated cheddar as extra, as though the overworked cooks don't have anything better to do than to grate some sunshine *queso* on his deluxe eggs. Menzies and I have a side bet on it this morning.

It's late March. Last night Harry took out his monstrous telescope and showed us the Horsehead Nebula and a star cluster in Orion's Belt. Harry likes stargazing and has a variety of devices for staring into the celestial spheres. This one was about the size of a lawn tractor, but portable. It's not just the size of the scope—which is really the size of its mirrors—it's the quality of the eyepiece, and he's got some rare and fine eyepieces and doesn't mind talking about them.

When the waitress comes around again Harry orders the Wonderwall Special, I opt for a Denver scramble, and Don Juan places his order, "Two eggs, please; wheat toast, no margarine; home fries, easy on the salt, please," and then he pauses for the golden moment.

"How would you like your eggs?"

"Scrambled . . . and could you grate . . . a . . . little . . . cheddar on them? Please."

Harry and I look at each other conspiratorially. Cha-ching.

"Helluva nice morning, really."

"Not much wind to speak of."

"Nope. Snow still up on the mountain. I heard some meadow-larks this morning—always a good sign. How are things down in the Fishbowl, Don Juan?"

"Pretty good," he says. "But I'm running into a bit of a problem with the collection."

"Which collection?"

"The arch collection . . ." He says it with a hard "k" sound. "*Arch* as in *archeology*."

He explains the difficult decision whether to move the archeological collection to a distant, centralized place. He lists a number of serious security issues related to its present location at an old house inside the national park: vandalism, rockslide, earthquake, fire, theft. He adds, "Law enforcement opens the locks and looks around once a week. All it would take is one smash-and-grab, one easy drive-by, and *pfft*, it's all gone. All those priceless pots and figurines, bye-bye. Gone. Forever."

He is in a pickle. "It's not as though you can just build a new building for the collection in the historic area, either," says Harry.

"No can do. No budget for that, of course. We've got to fund those wars, and no way to make it fit the historic fabric."

"Copy that. Inappropriate to historic fabric."

"What you gonna do about it?"

Don Juan takes a sip of water. "I'm going to have to deaccession the whole collection and move it to Tucson. It's part of our ongoing recertification plan."

" Deaccession?"

"Yes, deaccession."

"Tucson?"

"Tucson, as in Arizona?"

"Yep, Tucson. That's where the whole southwestern region's collections are stored . . ."

"Ongoing recertification plan?" I say.

"Ten-year cycle," he says. "Like accreditation. It never ends."

"I bet that hasn't made you real popular."

"No. You should hear what people have been saying on the phone. 'You sumbitch parkies—first you lock it up and kick out the cattle, then you tear down Fruita, and now you're going to send all *our* collection to goddamned Tucson, Arizona.'"

"Well, they've got a point there . . ."

"The locals do tend to have strong sediments."

"What about the researchers, the scholars?"

"Last year we had eight," Don Juan says. "Eight."

"Eight?"

"Eight, and they can still see the stuff in Tucson—in a climate-controlled, secure, centralized, state-of-the-art facility."

"I see your point there," says Harry.

"It's a bit out of context," I mention.

"And you don't think it's out of context in the Griffin House?"

"True enough. But it's catalogued as to where found, when, and by whom."

"It is," he says. "But it's not like you can take a pot out for the day, return it to its natural spot, and say, 'Behold the marvels of the Fremont Culture' and get all gooey over it."

"The Fremont Culture *or* the Anastassi," says Harry.

"Right, or surely the Anastassi," I say.

"The Anastassi *or* the Ancestral Puebloans."

"Bloody midget Anasazi," scowls Don Juan, looking away.

"'Those stasstistics about the disappearance of the Anastassi were fascinating, dear'—that's what they say in Boulder . . ."

"But no," says Harry. "It isn't going to make you real popular."

"No. So we're trying to keep it quiet."

"Don Juan, why don't you move those damned orchards to Tucson, too?"

"Longer growing season."

"Tucson, famous for peaches and apricots."

"Or the petroglyphs."

"Maybe the river could be diverted down there. They've got a mighty thirst for water."

"How 'bout moving Hickman Bridge?"

"The Golden Throne."

"Burro Wash, maybe."

"Cathedral Valley."

"South Desert."

"Funny."

"What's the superintendent say?"

"He says it's my call."

"Now there's some support. You stick your neck out, and it's your legacy, bro."

"Yeah."

Breakfast arrives.

Halfway through I lose my appetite and want to continue slicing up the history.

"What sort of name is Landy anyway, you might ask? Well, from what I heard, his real name is Randolph, shortened to Randy. But because his sister couldn't say 'Randy' with the speech impediment, the family went with Landy. Landy Covers.

"So Landy really liked to watch . . . When he built the Egyptian, with the low-interest government-provided loan, he had some special video cameras installed in a couple of rooms, including especially the Honeymoon Suite and the swimming pool ladies' dressing room. He had 'em piped into his private office, located above this very restaurant, and hell, nobody knew the difference. Security cameras, you know, for watching the front desk and parking lot—no monkey business around here—not at the Egyptian. Landy liked to wear one-piece jumpsuits and he liked to watch. Passed the time watching his guests . . . making sure they had a good time . . . making sure the swimming suits fit."

It was one of his disgruntled employees who ratted him out.

"Imagine this," I say. "You're on your wedding night at the best place around, getting frisky, and Landy Covers is up in his office enjoying the show—or at least taping it for tomorrow."

"Sick," says Harry.

"Gross, very gross," says Don Juan, scooping up some eggs with grated cheddar onto his naked toast.

"Troubling," adds Harry.

"So this disgruntled employee goes to the authorities, says, 'I found this hidden camera-thing in a light fixture and I thought you'd like to know.' They do a stakeout—can you imagine it—catch Landy red-handed, arrest him on his second serious morals charge, haul him off to jail. He posts bail, the story hits the Salt Lake news, it's bad for business, but they changed the venue.

Can't get a fair trial in Wayne County. The judge in Cedar City is his wife's second cousin, and he walks. He blames the disgruntled employee—said it was a setup—said he could prove that she was embezzling money . . . A maid embezzling money. Right, like she'd have access to the accounts . . .

"Everyone knew Landy favored one-piece jumpsuits, but in camo or brown, not orange, for huntin', you know, and nothing much unusual about that, though come to mention it, it does seem a bit strange, his hankering for the easy-zipping and easy-care jumpsuits . . . But when he made the evening news in an orange jumpsuit, on the second morals charge, there were some who felt that it was just, though it didn't stick."

"And he walked?" says Harry.

"He walked away, Renee . . . But he did have to sell the motel."

"Course by then he would've had it paid for," says Don Juan.

"Right. Paid for the motel with the low-interest loan and the video equipment with the profits."

"Are you sure they got rid of the cameras?" says Don Juan, looking around.

"I have it on good authority that they did."

"I wonder if they deaccessioned his collection?" says Harry.

"Probably kept is as evidence."

"Probably moved it to a central location."

"Probably are watching it right now."

"Oh, my stars!"

"I never liked eating breakfast at the Egyptian, anyway."

"Why not?"

"Those two eggs sunny side up always seemed to be staring at me—watching me . . . The Wonderwall is way better."

Burning Elvis

AT THE END OF DAY I LOVE TO STACK AND LIGHT AN OUTSIDE fire. My inner Boy Scout wants me to be the one to light it, to know that the ability to start a fire is an important survival skill, Rulon Gardner. The tending of it I'm happy to share. Somebody nearly always has an inner pyromaniac to feed: the need to stir with stick, to turn over half-burned logs and strike, sending sparks into the night, strike and stir again. Flames transform to coals if you let them, and in the coals evanesce the bittersweet beveled edges of summers past, lost in shimmering dance.

Over the years we've burned much in addition to wood: the annual winter prunings of the fruit trees, the grape canes, lots of weeds and grasses. A few years back I ceremoniously burned an external frame backpack I was sore at because it had failed me during a long walk in the Wind Rivers, broke down and busted apart right at the base of Vista Pass, not a good place for gear failure. By the way, backpack nylon burns for a surprisingly long time and makes a variety of neat colors on the way out. I showed that damned Jansport, didn't I? *Take that, New Green.* Jennifer and I have also done some ritualized effigial burning of our enemies.

To build a fire is to be twice warmed, Grasshopper. Or thrice. I keep my firewood in the woodpile. Snakes like it: shelter from the rain, warmth in the wind. Occasionally I've startled them and they in turn startled me. More often I've found their skins, revolting death-yellow moltings.

Sometimes we move into the woodpile to molt and shuffle off our skins. Garter snakes. Torporific. Soporific. Cinch-it-up-now.

I once found a garter snake curled around the seat hole of an antediluvian kayak I was just then trying to haul to the dump. It scared me—the snake, I mean. More recently, while grubbing around a grape and rebuilding a retaining wall, I found myself face-to-face with a garter serpent, ugly sullen gray thing. I like neither spiders nor snakes.

Spiders, snakes, and mice come with living in the pastures. So does the shed.

In the end, what to do with the it?

(1) Jennifer thinks we should burn it, just get rid of it, give up on it.

I'm okay with that.

When Harry Menzies bought his old-time place, it came with a dirt-floored, rat-infested shed too far gone to salvage, and he burned it down to ash. Scott Chestnut brought the town fire truck over and kept in running, raked up a bouffant of ragweed, tossed a match on it, and watched it burn. Throughout the day the bonfire burned and smoldered. Folks from all over town brought their combustibles by. *Hey, would you mind if I tossed this in?* A useful pyre.

I could probably do the same thing. It would certainly feel good to watch it tumble and watch it burn.

But to entrust any sort of thing to the Good Water volunteer fire department, or any of the other hosers of Wayne County, would be a foolish. Their competence is easy to question. I understand that the fire marshal is a bit of a serpent himself and crooked as a dog's hind leg. He shakes people down to pad his personal budget.

(2) Also, that smoldering vision bothers my sense of entropy. There's still plenty of dimensional lumber to reuse and some weatherworn planks. Demolition is much easier and faster than building, but the effort required to build should not be forgotten. Demolition is fool's work—that's why one likes it. Demolition is low-skilled labor. Hell, I have the kind of friends who might like a demo party: pass out the gloves, protective glasses, earplugs, beer, crowbars, sledges. Blood may be drawn but hopefully not splattered. There is no measuring, no reason to worry about level and plumb, just pound and pry and yank, Hank.

Demolition with an eye to recycling, now, that's a better way to do it.

(3) On the other hand, why tear it down, why burn it? Jennifer alternatively thinks we should fix it up and add onto it. Lord knows we need more shed space. Why not let it stand but improve it? With a little time and trouble: fix up the cracks, jack up that one corner, put a new roof on, maybe a new window, perhaps a store-bought door, then haul everything out and just hose it down before restocking. That's a solution that makes sense. Life doesn't give a person sheds without number. I'm not twenty-seven any more. Why waste the work? Why not find a use for the refuse and memories?

So instead of burning the shed, we decided to burn Elvis. Not Elvis Elvis, Elvis Aaron Presley, of course, but our six-foot-high cardboard Elvis in gold lamé. The figure of Elvis. His image. His representation. For ten years it had stood guard in various places around the place and had faded quite a bit. A faded King had lost its luster.

Thus, on a milepost birthday, the Elvis pyre was properly prepared. Winter-dried branches piled up. His music blasting on CD. A few thank ya, thank ya very muches. Then match to fibrous, and all went up in flames. And then Elvis left the building.

All except the Elvis smile. The ebony locks and movie star face burned black and curled back, but the smile—I swear it—it wouldn't burn. The King's dreamy dentition just lay on the coals a-grinning at us. Spooky. One has to be careful with such things.

The shed has stood these twenty-plus years. The shed has served its purpose. Keep what you can and reuse. Value what you have. Burn the rest. Keep a pail of water close in case it gets out of hand.

To Remember What Is Lost

1.

MUSIC IS AS MUCH ABOUT SILENCE AS VIBRATION, he liked to say, the space in between. And if you're going to say it, say it in three parts, in three keys, in triptych. Don't oversay it. That was Ken Brewer—minimalist to the end: less is more, but really less is never quite enough.

Ken taught three things: pay attention, make every word count, and practice your chops. As teacher he was a little less minimalist and elaborated these and other concepts in Socratic ways. He took me under his wing. I was lucky to have Ken as a mentor at the right time, just as he was fortunate to have Keith Wilson.

Good graces meant breakfasts together—at L.D.'s in Richmond, at Angies in Logan. Since he was an institution in Cache Valley, he'd nod or wave to half the people in the room. We talked about the challenges of our stepdaughters, about our wives, the mother-daughter deal. We talked about sending things out and puffing up our pride.

It came to this. Kenneth W. Brewer, the poet laureate of the state of Utah, stopped by our house in Green River, Wyoming, in June 2005, on his way back from a writers' conference in Cheyenne. He was feeling ill. It was like him to be feeling ill. A burly bear of a man who looked like Pavarotti and liked to conduct with his left hand while reading his poetry, still, any cold laid him low. In his Old Man phase, the fifteen years I knew him, he was not afraid to enumerate the petty ailments of the flesh and milk them. Ken was actually a bit of a hypochondriac. So we assumed this was just a case of the flu.

He stopped by on the way home because Jennifer was his step-daughter, and he always liked to talk to Jennifer, for she is good to talk to, and he had been married to Jennifer's mother, Bobbie Stearman, off and on for thirty years. He stopped in because he liked having a reason to. All along the hell-and-gone stretch of I80, it's good to have something to look forward to.

Two weeks later, Jennifer called from Bryce Canyon to check in. The diagnosis was simple, bad, and there was no mistake in it. Pancreatic cancer, terminal, two or three months to live. In the ensuing numbered days he taught each of us who knew him, respected him, loved him, what it is you do when you receive your sentence.

They gave him three months. He borrowed ten.

What a graceful exit it would prove to be. Every day he tried to practice what mattered. He wrote poems, received visitors, and watched the birds. He made the *CBS Evening News*. Always the teacher, he modeled how it is you die.

The end came on the ides of March 2006. Jennifer was there because he asked her to be. She was iron. He knew her to be the strongest woman in his life. He got his wish to die at home in the mountainous lap of Providence. Providence, Utah. The moon, just past full, rose among vellum clouds.

2

Plenty of poets are teachers but not good ones, and some teachers are poets, but Ken was both. To say "teacher" is only part of it. Ken was also a mentor.

As I've said, what Ken mentored was simple enough: make every word count, practice your chops, and listen to the sounds of words, wind, and your heart. That's easy to say. Method matters more. Ken showed many the keys to the woodshed, the hantavirus shed, and showed how to store things there, move them around, and clean them up.

When it came time for me to end my apprenticeship and stand on my own stilts, I still wanted him to be critical and editorial and helpful, but he would not do it. Everything was good. Everything was interesting. I had to find it myself. Feel the Force, Luke.

So today when I get things right, I hear him. Sometimes I hear him saying my words aloud, or laughing, or shaking his head when it's not there yet.

I see those dark eyes. I watch him leading that imaginary orchestra. I remember him worrying every word.

And when the words will not come or come out badly, missing the mark, I see Ken staring out a window, studying the birds and trees and gray-shadowed hills of Cache Valley.

I see him, too, a lonely boy in Indianapolis, raised by his grandmother, the chronic angers of his parents' house, and I praise this country and the glories of public education, that a boy whose parents ran a trucking company could grow up to be a poet and professor. And I praise the chance that came his way to go to New Mexico State on a football scholarship, and how he met his mentor, Keith Wilson, who also taught by precept, sure, but mainly through silence. Ken glommed onto Keith and convinced him to read his first year's work, and throughout that early time, Keith said nearly nothing and shouldn't have. Teach through silence. Learn through trial and error. At some point we must be alone to shout—or sing—above the wind, the rattle of this mortal wind, as Ken would say: the only wind we know.

The only wind we need to know.

3.

July 2004. Some years a fire restriction works against a desire for bonfires and fireworks. You can't really be a scofflaw in town—it's too visible. These are not good times in Good Water, though restrictions probably prevent grass fires. On wetter years, the authorities loosen up a bit and allow the populace to affirm and indulge the practice of freedom.

July 4th is Good Water's red-letter day. Allegedly the date of first settlement, in 1888, the annual "Apple Days" celebration begins with a double-dip parade up and back down Highway 24, Main Street. The parade features drummers and fifers, cheerleaders from the high school, antique cars, roaring motorcycles, one or more equestrian groups, trailers full of cute kids, fire trucks from various agencies, a few homemade floats from local businesses, and the Grand Marshal or Marchioness (one of the oldest ambulatory people in the county) waving a flag or sometimes sleeping in the back seat of a fancy old car. The parade is followed by the flea market, the quilt show, the barbeque lunch, and eventually the dance.

As darkness falls, pickups from all over south-central Utah will stream into town to the Big Apple (named for the old-time orchards) dance pavilion to whoop, holler, and cut it up to country or country-rock bands. "Sweet Home Alabama" will surely be heard, probably twice, occasionally thrice, as will "Mustang Sally," "Proud Mary," "Heard it in a Love Song," and "Freebird."

During and after the dance, fireworks are discharged in many locations, sometimes putting to the test the fire trucks seen earlier in the day at the parade, and the entire effort is a glorious celebration of Americana.

—

I had bought me some kick-ass Wyoming fireworks and saved them for such a special occasion. The fire had died down to the hippie TV level and shimmering coals quavered in the night breeze. The fireworks needed to be sent up before the moon rose. I lit the first ones, bottle rockets on steroids, and they whooshed up, fiery streamers, making dramatic *pows* against the dark scrim. Giddy with success, more were sent up into the star-spangled ink, curving against it, fine sprigs of bright bold color. And mister, if you prefer peace and quiet, then you better avoid Good Water, Utah, on the Fourth of July.

Hear the cowboy band, the seething lines of cow folk hooting and hollering, the various fireworks, the roar of angry pickups, the toot of horns. Howdy, pardner, welcome to the country—this here's freedom.

Ken was leaning over on his chair and smiling at all this, not saying much. Silence was the best response to spectacle. Each time a new one blasted up and was swept east by the prevailing—and you can actually see the Milky Way up there—he uttered a "mmmmmmm" of approval. Somehow they reminded me of little spermatozoa swimming up into the fallopian tubes of night, searching for an egg to pince and join onto, an observation I shared. He leaned sideways and laughed, said he was thinking exactly the same thing.

The fire pit was shaped like a bloated keyhole, lined and ringed with andesite rocks, and it enabled a very fine and controlled bonfire, an excellent place for cooking with a narrowed slot in the upstream end that accommodates two grills very nicely, with ponderosa, fir, spruce, and perhaps just a dash of cedar.

One time around this fire pit, and I cannot remember the exact year, but several of the Good Water ne'er-do-wells were lingering and malingering around the fire pit and it was raining lightly and the moon was fully up and in the darkened night sky there ranged a moonbow—an arc of moonshine gently illuminated and stretching in the lightly falling rain. And I have stood and sat beside many a fire in my days and have never seen another moonbow. Now, rainbows are a weekly occurrence in season, doubles being just as common and nothing that remarkable, but to see that arc in gray-black misty night is not something to forget but to remember, we lucky few. I mention this to Ken and he says, "Oh, yeah. That would be something to see."

There is no harm in fireworks. The dousing hose is running on the nearby golden delicious apple tree. Not one of us can imagine that in eighteen months Ken will be gone or that his ashes will be joined with the waters of the Logan River, at Brown's Pour Off, a stream he knew well and fished and sang of, ever-changing.

4.

In the morning he will write this poem in our guests' journal.

WATERING THE BUSHES IN GOOD WATER, UTAH, 7/3/04
—For Christopher

Christopher watered the bushes,
his bare behind bright
beyond the bonfire,
then went to bed in his room,
second story of the Good Water house.

Later that night, I too
watered the bushes, discreet
in the bright full moon,
memories of my father
on the Tippecanoe River
nearly sixty years ago,
showing me how,
"left hand on your hip,
right hand on your hose."

Behind us, the mighty bonfire
flared, sassafras popping,
flames rising, sparks.
After all these years,
it's one lesson I learned
and still remember.

Acknowledgments

Earlier versions of these chapters appeared in the following publications: "Moving Water," *Post Road;* "Town Owl," *Tiny Lights;* "Blue and Gray," *Junction;* "Burning Fields," *Wyoming Fence Lines;* "Reliquary," *Petroglyph;* "Two Chairs," *Rough Draft;* "Wild Currants," *Timberline;* "High Plateau Blues," *Weber Studies;* "The Mighty Blizzard of 1995," *Red Rock Review;* "South Wind from the West," *Manzanita;* "National Monuments," *Junction.*

"Cedar and Stone" appears in *Small Scenes,* published by Limberlost Press, 2006.